EARRINGS in the CELLAR

Growing Up in Ruined Worlds

Rachel Bernheim

Translated from the Hebrew by
Anthony Berris and Miriam Talisman

Typesetting: Pardes Publishing House
Cover Design: Studio Paz, Jerusalem
Photo on front cover: Zeev Bernheim's garden of statues

ISBN 9789652293343

1 3 5 7 9 8 6 4 2

Gefen Publishing House
6 Hatzvi Street, Jerusalem 94386, Israel
972-2-538-0247 • orders@gefenpublishing.com

Gefen Books
600 Broadway, Lynbrook ,NY 11563, USA
1-800-477-5257 • orders@gefenpublishing.com

www.israelbooks.com

Printed in Israel

Send for our free catalogue

In memory of

My dear mother and father,
My sister Ada'leh.
My brother Shlomo
And my relatives who are no more.
We shall remember
The parents, the children
And the aged
Whose lives were cut off
Because they were Jews.

… I left there, never to return,
I didn't even want to go back.
My past that I did not love
Has again become my beloved past.
… As if our world is not in ruins,
As if we shall never know all we do,
As if our home and place still stand
A white table set for a meal.

My Old Home
Leah Goldberg

Contents

Chapter One	My Family Home	1
Chapter Two	Childhood and Youth	13
Chapter Three	Under Hungarian Rule	31
Chapter Four	In the Ghetto	45
Chapter Five	Auschwitz-Birkenau	53
Chapter Six	Forced Labor	67
Chapter Seven	Sabotage	73
Chapter Eight	Escape from the Death March	77
Chapter Nine	In a German Village	87
Chapter Ten	Lost Days	107
Chapter Eleven	Cyprus	125
Chapter Twelve	Israel	131

My Family Home

I was born on June 4, 1922, to my father, Ya'akov Friedman, and my mother, Matilda (née Munch), after my two brothers, Eliezer, the eldest, and Shlomo.

Less than two years later, on February 4, my sister Chaya was born, and she was followed six years later by our sister Ada, my parents' youngest child. Our family of seven was considered small in those days; all around us were families of ten or more children.

The town where I was born, Mukachevo, as the Czechs called it, or Munkács in Hungarian, lies on the eastern border of what used to be the Czechoslovakian Republic. Immediately following the First World War, the country was divided into several regions: Czechoslovakia with its capital Prague; Moravia-Silesia whose capital was Brno; Slovakia and its capital Bratislava; and finally there was Carpatorus, that the Russians call Carpathian Russia. Officially, the town of Ozhorod was the district capital, but from the economic, municipal, and cultural standpoints, Mukachevo was considered to be the principal town.

Our area was notable for its variety, in all senses of the word. First the landscape, the Carpathian Mountains that were covered with green trees all year round. Forests, fields, and numerous flowing rivers, like the Laturice River that crossed our town, whose waters, like those of all the other rivers in the area, flowed southward to the Blue Danube.

Like the landscape, the population, too, was varied. There were the older generations, who had remained in the area since the time of the Austro-Hungarian empire, and spoke German and Hungarian, and there were numerous minorities from the neighboring countries with which we shared a common border—Poland to the north, the Ukraine and Russia to the east, Romania and Hungary in the south—and our Jewish brethren, of course.

In my time the number of Jews in our town was almost half of the total population, 17,000 of the 37,000 inhabitants, covering the entire spectrum of European Jewry. Some had assimilated and moved away from Judaism; there were Zionists from all the various streams and movements; and the religious Jews, who were also divided amongst themselves. Each rabbi had his own court and followers. Some were extremely radical, like those known today as the Satmar *hasidim*, a number of which came to Israel and live today in the Meah She'arim quarter of Jerusalem.

There was much dissension and rivalry between the various religious factions, a rivalry that was more bitter even than their opposition to the Zionists, who they considered worse than the Gentiles. If one of the rabbis' courts was short of a tenth male for the prayer quorum, the congregants would go out into the street and look for a Jew, rather than invite a member of a neighboring rabbi's court.

Our central European climate was also varied. The year was divided into four seasons, almost exactly to the day on the calendar. The spring thawed the snow, and the bluebells, the first flowers to peep from the earth's white blanket, heralded the new season. They were the first to flower, enchanting in their special beauty, and were followed by a carpet of all shades of green, mixed with large flowery patches, that covered the earth as far as the eye could see.

In the summer the abundant fruit ripened, and in the gardens the blackberry bushes and mulberry trees were full. Cherries filled the market stalls. When I was a child I was happy that my birthday fell in June, at the height of the fruit season, when cherries were cheap and we would eat them and hang them from our ears in pairs like earrings. There was so much fruit—plums, apples, and pears, the most noble of which was called *Kaiser Birne* (King Pear). Each bite dripped sweet juice and the taste was unforgettable.

I didn't know my grandparents. My father's parents died before I was born and I only knew two of his sisters: petite Auntie Feigeleh (Zipporah), whose shrunken face was deeply lined, and roly-poly Auntie Teibeleh (Yona), in whose deep-set eyes I always saw a smile. We used to visit Auntie Zipporah when we were children just to satisfy our parents, but it was an unpleasant chore. She was what the Jews called *bazditnetzeh*, a woman with no children, barren, but the term was used to describe a woman who had no affection for children. Perhaps this was why Zipporah was extremely orderly and pedantic, and we used to say that she had an obsession for cleanliness. We were poor, and Mother rarely baked cakes, except for once a year before the Purim festival, so that we would be able to reciprocate when we were brought *Mishloah Manot*, Purim gifts of cakes and baked goods, a widespread custom on this festival. Throughout the day, we were visited, as was every Jewish house, by entertainers who would perform the *Purimspiel*, a Purim parody in rhyme, and they would be paid for their efforts with cakes. Our neighbors, friends, and acquaintances brought us *Mishloah Manot*, and Mother would assemble trays of baked goods to give in return, a mixture of cakes that she had baked herself, together with some we had received.

At Purim we went to visit Auntie Zipporah, and she stood over us as we ate the cake she offered us. The first time, I thought that she wanted to see how we were enjoying her cake, but then I would become disappointed, each time anew, because I had forgotten what she was like. She would bend over and pick up every crumb that dropped from our mouths or hands, and because we were so frightened of her, we dropped crumbs all the time.

In contrast, I very much enjoyed visiting Auntie Yona, who always had a warm welcome for us. She wasn't wealthy, but she was a good woman, always happy to see us. She told us to eat, but made sure that her husband wouldn't see. He wasn't a miser but she felt uncomfortable when he saw how "wasteful" she was, because they barely made a living. He was an impressive-looking man, large in stature, with a red beard. He was very talented, too, and composed songs and tunes that he would sing with a fine voice. He was well known in the Jewish community and was invited to entertain at weddings and other celebrations. Auntie Yona had a heart of gold and always had something for us to eat, standing at our side persuading us to taste her *lekach*, a confection usually reserved for weddings, and all the other delicacies she baked and of which she was justly proud.

My mother and father came from very religious families. The institution of the *shadchan*, the matchmaker, was accepted then and without it young girls would not meet boys before marriage. When Father reached the marriageable age of eighteen, the matchmakers began calling at his parents' house with recommendations for a good match. Father rejected all the comely brides and the daughters of wealthy families they offered, and sent the matchmakers to my mother's house. He remembered her after seeing her once by chance, standing in front of a shop window that reflected her face. He moved away but was drawn back to her. A few days later he returned to the shop and saw her again. He looked at her once more, and was sure that he would meet only her beneath the wedding canopy.

A very short time after the matchmaker approached my mother, my parents were married in a religious ceremony. It was love at first sight. My mother was a very beautiful woman of average height, with a shy smile, and lovely blue eyes. She had a good figure and her chestnut hair fell in thick waves. Father was half a head taller than her, his expression serious, with slightly prominent cheekbones, and above his brown eyes were thick eyebrows that met above his nose. He wore a hat like all the young men of the time and his side-locks curled down from his temples onto his cheeks. Before the wedding, Mother was forced to part with her beautiful, luxuriant hair. Her head was shaved and she tied a kerchief gracefully over her wig.

During my childhood I heard no details of the early days of their marriage. They lived together for only a very short time, less than a year, before they were forced to separate. The bullet fired in Sarajevo that killed Archduke Ferdinand, the scion of the Austro-Hungarian dynasty, was the opening shot and on the first of August, 1914, World War I broke out. The billboards announced a general mobilization and Father said goodbye to Mother and went off to the war. Three days later, on the fourth of August, my elder brother Eliezer was born. Communications were still underdeveloped and Mother did not know how to inform her husband that he was the father of a son. World War I was very different from the wars of modern times—the armies were formed in battle lines, fighting along a wide front somewhere far away. Mother had no address through which to inform my father of the news, but she was happy that at least in the matter of the name there was no problem. Unlike the majority of religious couples, they talked about everything, and with regard to the name there was no room for uncertainty. Before Father left home they agreed that if the baby was a boy, he would be named Eliezer.

Father left for the war on a train packed with young men who had been called up to serve. He sat on a bench next to another young man who, like Father, twisted his side-locks into a narrow curl that he put behind his ears under his army cap. Father took a liking to him right away as he seemed to be sociable and liked to talk. They introduced themselves and immediately became friends. As they talked, they realized that apart from their side-locks and army caps, they had something else in common. They had both left behind wives in an advanced stage of pregnancy and the birth was expected any day. The two new friends were very happy for one another and shook hands in the Jewish way of slapping their palms together, as if sealing a bargain. This custom was widely accepted at the time and was a kind of unwritten agreement, yet one that was binding, like a vow. They agreed that if the new babies would be of different sex, they would be betrothed to each other in marriage by virtue of their handshake.

When they returned home at the end of the war, it became clear that the agreement could not be kept, and there were many reasons for this "breach of contract." The most decisive reason was that Father came home from the war a different man. He returned with a progressive worldview and was full of plans for the future, while his friend from the train remained the same conservative, narrow-minded Jew he had always been. My father later discovered that, as a young man, his friend had not found his feet in the city and had gone back to the village where he was born, married his wife, who bore him four girls, all raised as observant Jews. They were obedient and their father was proud of them since they were all excellent professional seamstresses. When they had reached marriageable age, they sat at home, sewing from morn till night, and between the clothes they made they waited for the *shadchan* to bring them a good match.

After the war, the two erstwhile friends lived in different worlds, and the handshake-promise was never mentioned. Over the years he would come to town and visit us, and I can remember him from one of those visits when I was still a little girl. They maintained a friendly relationship, but no more.

This friend could see how different he and my father were and expressed no anger towards my father, who had broken the agreement between them. He knew that the promised match between the two young people who had grown up in such different worlds—his seamstress daughter on the one hand, and my brother, who was already an outstanding student at the Gymnasium on the other—would never come to fruition.

My mother, who had been left alone at home after my father was drafted into the army, only heard about the agreement between the two friends many years later.

The war went on. Father was in the army and Mother was alone. She was a very industrious woman who did all the housework briskly and took care of my brother, who was starting to walk. She also bore the burden of making a living for them both by taking on work she could do at home, and this she did in every free moment she had. By the light of an oil lamp she sewed buttons onto army uniforms that were brought to her from the factory, and collected when they were finished. She would quietly hum a lullaby as she rocked my baby brother's cradle with her foot, and nimbly sewed. Day and night, Mother labored to earn a living for her baby son and herself. She did it all quietly, living in the hope that one day her husband would come home on leave and how happy he would be to see her and his son. Day after day she looked forward to his coming, but he did not appear, and she was worried because so far she had received no word of him.

Some of the young men who had evaded conscription and not gone to the war would talk derisively of those who had, only to be killed. They bragged that it wasn't for them because they liked having a "good time." Various suitors came to Mother's house every day bringing her bad news from the war, each report worse than the previous one. They told her about bloody battles and the numerous dead and wounded, with the sole objective of persuading Mother to marry them. They told her that she was wasting her best years waiting for Father who, in all probability, would never return. The war went on and they continued to pester my mother with their nagging: why did she have to work so hard? If she married one of them they promised her anything she wanted, to take care of her and her son—just as long as she agreed to marry them. Mother held her own with honor and was never tempted. She was convinced of what her heart told her, that one day, her husband would come back to her alive and well. The moment she looked at her son, my brother Eliezer, the tears in her eyes were banished as she saw him smiling at her. From his adoring eyes she drew strength, and her belief in her husband's return was strengthened. On Eliezer's third birthday, he was placed in a high chair with Mother holding him from behind, watching the *galach*, the barber, giving him his first haircut. She watched as the beautiful golden curls dropped to the floor, in accordance with the religious precept, just like any other three-year-old boy from a religious family.

One day, many months after Father's departure, a soldier on furlough, who had come straight from the front, arrived at Mother's house with a letter for her. She thanked him and was very excited and as soon as the messenger had departed, she put the baby in his cradle, covered him, and read the letter excitedly, a smile spreading over her face, tears of joy filling her eyes. She read it and reread it and only later bent down to pick up the photograph that had fallen from the envelope as she opened it. It was a picture of a soldier wearing a *rubashka* buttoned up to the neck, breeches that flared to the knees (like those worn by cavalrymen), holding the reins of a saddled horse that stood by his side. Mother looked at the photograph for a long time. She held her head in her hands, shook it sadly from side to side, vainly searching for her husband in the picture until she realized that the man was not him. "The address must have been changed" she thought. This man was not the young scholar from whom she had parted at the beginning of the war.

Throughout that day she was confused, kissing her little son, and clasping him to her bosom. Late in the evening, after she had laid my brother down to sleep in his cradle, she finished her housework, sewed on the last of the buttons for the day, and went to bed, her feelings in turmoil. She took the envelope from under her pillow and looked at the photograph again. This time she ignored his strange clothing and looked straight into Father's eyes. A scream burst from deep within her. This time she was sure that it was him, her husband. She looked again at the photograph in her trembling hand. Who was this man, holding the horse's reins, the man who looked like a reckless Gentile? But she knew that it must be her husband. All night she moved between sleep and wakefulness, looking at the photograph again and again, looking straight into Father's eyes, her heartbeat reverberating through her and anxiety invading her heart.

The war was well into its fourth year. Very few came home for a short leave and told stories of the situation at the front, which appeared to be optimistic, and there were those who believed that the war would be over shortly and the soldiers would return home.

Mother, who throughout this period had looked forward expectantly to her husband's return, told my brother Eliezer about the father he had never met; that on the day he, Eliezer, was born, he was far away because of the war. She told him that, thank God, they were both lucky because many of the men who had gone to war had not come back. But it was their good fortune, she told him, that his father was alive and well and in a few weeks' time, or even a few days' time, he would be coming home to them and they would be together like any other family. She told her son again and again that his father was a hero and that he should be proud of him. She prepared him for the meeting with the father he did not know, but she never thought of herself for a moment, or of her impending reunion with her beloved husband.

The door opened and a handsome man stood in the doorway , his hair thick on his bare head—for observant Jews to be without a head covering was expressly forbidden. To my mother, Father looked like a complete stranger. This was not the man she had known. He seemed fatigued, his uniform mud-spattered. He put down the big wooden box, which served as a suitcase, in the doorway, and the moment he did so he looked joyously into his wife's eyes, opened his arms to embrace her and saw that she remained where she was. From the sheer surprise of seeing him she stood still, watching, stunned, while Father's eyes were locked with hers. Mother simply stood there, unresponsive, as though paralyzed, her feet rooted to the floor, not moving.

Surprised and disappointed by her reaction, he saw his little son, and said joyfully, "Come here, my sweet little boy, come and get a kiss from your father." My brother was clinging to my mother's dress and then he wrapped his arms around her legs with all his strength, his refuge from this strange man. He was generally a shy boy and now he wanted to hide, as he did whenever a stranger came into the house. My mother caressed him, her feet still rooted to the same spot, unable to move.

She slowly managed to collect herself, and said in her soft, motherly voice, encouraging my brother, "Go on, son, go my sweet, say hello to your father. He's come back to us from the war." My brother refused and hung back, and only with my mother's help approached Father, step by step, and stood by his side, his eyes downcast. Father was careful not to frighten him. All the time he was far from home, he had imagined his homecoming, dreaming of the joy of being reunited with his wife and son whom he had thought about throughout the years of the war. But mentally he was unprepared for what awaited him, the estrangement that hurt him so much. He was very sad and to hide his tears from the boy he bent down to open his army footlocker. My brother moved closer and stood at his side, watching him take a package from the box, seeing his nimble fingers untie the string around a leather pouch from which he took a reindeer with big antlers, a bear, and all kinds of other creatures that the little boy, who lived closed up in the house with his mother, had never seen before. My father had carved these wonderful animals with his own hands, using only a penknife, during his four-and-a-half years as a prisoner of war. It is doubtful that when he carved the animals he thought that the day would come when they would help to dissolve the barriers between him and his son.

Among the many things that Father made in the prison camp was a carved chess set. I remember the rook, somewhat reminiscent of one of the towers of Jerusalem, ornately carved—a true work of art. Father had managed to keep the chess set intact during the long period until his return. The rook had a place of honor at home; it stood on an embroidered doily that covered the sideboard, and it aroused the amazement of everyone who saw it.

Over his many years in captivity Father made friends with several educated and cultured people to whom he listened, with interest, and very quickly became part of their "school." One might say that my father was the perfect autodidact and during his captivity underwent a radical change. From the religious scholar who curled his side-locks and prayed and who, aside from prayer, had no interests at all, he became a complete heretic who denied the existence of God. Over the years, he became more open and aware of what was happening around him, and by the time he returned home at the end of the war, he had formulated a worldview with clear, radical Left leanings.

I loved Saturday evenings. We used to sit by the light of the oil lamp that cast shadows on the walls, and listen to my father's wonderful, captivating stories. It was on one of those evenings that we heard about the many problems my parents had encountered upon my father's return. We listened to stories about those early days when Mother and Father, who had been separated for four and a half years, felt like complete strangers. We heard of Mother's efforts to get used to her "new" husband. Mother was still an observant Jew who adhered to all the religious precepts, while Father was a man of the world. They loved each other very much and Father was patient with Mother. It was thanks to his sound attitude towards her and their son that they managed to break the ice between them and establish a wonderful relationship, and slowly, step by step, he won her over.

In the early days, he would go outside on Saturdays, the Sabbath day, to smoke his cigarettes in private, out of respect and consideration for Mother, who still observed the Sabbath laws. She accepted this habit but was still concerned. "What will the neighbors say?" Yet Mother slowly began to accept her new husband and was even happy.

A few months later, after some difficult deliberations, she gave up wearing a wig like every married Jewish woman, and let her chestnut-colored hair grow. She plaited it in a thick braid and rolled it like a garland on top of her head.

I loved to hear Mother tell about the first night after Father's return, how she made their double bed after sleeping in it alone for so many nights, and how she felt—and here she blushed deeply—when he held her in his arms and covered her face with kisses, the taste of which she had not experienced in the past.

My parents suffered greatly with my father's return. He was a stranger in his environment, among the Orthodox Jews, and even his pre-war friends turned their backs on him. Friends kept their distance, the neighbors no longer accepted Mother in their midst, but what caused my parents the greatest sorrow was the suffering of their little boy, Eliezer. Every day he would come home from *heder* in tears and it was only after much persuasion that he admitted that the other children were mocking him because of Father, who wasn't like the other fathers and who didn't even wear the traditional Orthodox Jew's hat, the *streimel*. One day Eliezer returned home bruised and bleeding. Father did not hesitate for a moment, and said he would not send his son to the *heder* any longer. From then on he took Eliezer's education into his own hands. This news of my father, a heretic who denied the existence of God, spread like wildfire around the community. Mother suffered in silence, Father gritted his teeth, knowing that he had brought this situation upon them, and it caused him great sorrow. The vengeance of my mother's family was not long in coming. Without warning they all came to say goodbye to her, holding the affidavit and other documents for their passage to the *Goldene Medina*, America, to which the Jews at that time aspired to emigrate. Like thieves in the night, our relatives had their photographs taken and readied their documents, and the day before they were to sail, they came to say goodbye. Some years later, fully aware of my parents' dire financial straits and to ease their pangs of conscience, these relatives occasionally sent packages containing clothing, canned food, and letters with a few dollars inside.

This went on for many years and once contact between us had been reestablished, they wanted to send me packages, too. I wrote them a letter of thanks, saying that I lived in a kibbutz and wasn't short of a thing, but my aunt, who had heard of the shortages in Israel, insisted and carried on sending the packages, so I handed them over to the kibbutz clothes store, or the "commune" as we called it. At home, I never heard an expression of sorrow or regret about the split between our family and my mother's family that had been caused by my father.

We loved weekend evenings, sitting by the light of the oil lamp whose flame danced on the walls as we listened to Father telling us about bitter battles between two cavalry battalions. He described them in great detail, so much so that I could actually see the noble horses and their cavalrymen riders sinking to their deaths in the foul morass. And once we heard about a battle in which the two forces stood at the ready, facing one another: the Russian army and the Austrian army, in which my father served. The battle was fierce and in those days, before the advent of the sophisticated weaponry used by modern armies, the soldiers fought hand to hand. They were drawn up in formation, one mass of soldiers facing a similar mass of the enemy, when suddenly, at the height of the fighting and before my father's very eyes, an enemy soldier fell to the ground and died, with the words *Shema Yisrael* on his lips. Realizing that he was a Jew just like him, Father was stunned. The thought gave him no rest. "What have I done," he asked himself. He had killed a Jew with his own hands, just because he was wearing the uniform of the opposing army. Father never said so, but in retrospect it is entirely possible that at that very moment, for the first time, he conducted a moral stocktaking that led to the fateful turning point in his way of thinking and worldview.

Father fought for four years until he was severely wounded near the heavily fortified Faschmissel Castle. He and his comrades fought valiantly; food and ammunition supplies did not reach them and they were cut off. Many died from cold and hunger, or in the bloody battles, in one of which Father was wounded, losing consciousness and finding himself a prisoner of war when he came to. And so for him, the war ended. As an adult, I was told of one of his most moving experiences after his return from the war. It was a Saturday morning and my parents were still in bed talking, as was their custom, when for the first time since Father returned, my brother slowly got into their bed and lay down between them. Joyfully, Father hugged and kissed him and in return was rewarded with his son's first hesitant but sweet kiss.

Mother with my brother Eliezer

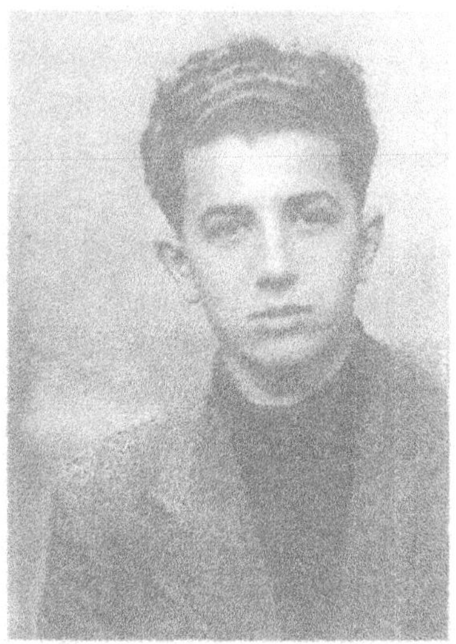

My brother Shlomo

Father in the Russian captivity, 1917

CHAPTER TWO

Childhood and Youth

My earliest childhood memories take me back to my father's workbench, which was covered with various-sized boxes filled with nails and wooden pegs of every shape and kind. I loved sorting and rearranging the nails in their boxes. The bench was small; the files, chisels, and other tools that hung from both sides fascinated me.

I would sit on a stool beside my father and follow his swift movements. In particular I liked watching him make elegant shoes for wealthy ladies, because they were custom made. He would adjust the wooden last, a skill in itself, to each shoe, add a piece of leather to make a larger shoe, or remove some for a smaller one. He made his living mainly by making the heavy work boots he sold to the peasants, who wore them for work on the farm; they had to be strong and durable for working in the mud. Payment for making a pair of work boots was meager, but the work was not time-consuming.

My father used wooden pegs for making these sturdy farmer's boots. I preferred watching him make the elegant women's shoes, the soles of which were hand stitched. I followed all the stages, from his preparation of the strong, thin waxed threads, waiting for the moment Father would begin to sew. His mouth would then be free of the wooden pegs he used to hold between his teeth, a time-saving device. When he began to sew, his mouth free of the pegs, he could sing. He loved singing; he had a mellifluous voice and perfect pitch. Other times he would tell me a story.

The flavor of some of these songs, and particularly his *meises* (little stories), are still with me, even today. One of them was about a wealthy man:

"In the old days all the Jews who could afford it, even those who were not rich, would invite a young single man, either without family or poor, to their homes, to join the family for the Friday night meal. Friday mornings all the Jews would go to the *mikvah* (ritual bath)—for many it was their only bath of the week. In the *mikvah* all were equal—naked as the day they were born—"in the image of God." One day two young yeshiva students met at the *mikvah*; one told the other of a wealthy man, and warned him that despite his being one of the richest men in town, he was one of the stingiest. It would be better for him to know this in advance so that when they served him fish broth and *hallah*, he should not forget that and exploit the opportunity to the full and eat as much as he could, because his hosts would offer nothing else to guests of his kind.

"In the *mikvah* all are equal, and no one knows who is who, since everyone is naked. Once the miserly well-off man was bathing next to these two young men, and was astonished when he heard their conversation. He stood with his back to them and heard every word they said. He was livid at the public compromising of his reputation, when a brilliant idea struck him, and he knew how he would teach his "guest" a lesson.

"On Friday the young man appeared. The wealthy man greeted him with *Shabbat Shalom* and invited him to join the family at the table. His wife covered her face and blessed the candles. The wealthy man poured wine into the glasses and ordered the servant to serve the guest with fish broth and braided *hallah*. Remembering what he had heard at the *mikvah*, the young man broke off a piece of *hallah* and dipped it in the fish broth. When he finished the *hallah* he was served a new one. When he finished the fish broth the cheerful servant brought him another bowl. The young man continued to break off more and more *hallah*, dipping it in the broth and eating. He remained in his chair, feeling like a stuffed goose, his stomach a balloon ready to burst at any moment, and he was unable to budge. While he was resting in his chair the servant came out of the kitchen with a pot of "golden" soup, *kneidlach* swimming in a clear chicken broth. Another servant followed and the smell of roast meat wafted through the air. The young man's salivary glands set to work. Another young servant followed with a tray heaped with puddings, the like of which he had never seen or tasted before. His nostrils widened, he swallowed his saliva, but could not touch any of the delicacies …"

And another little story: "A poor and destitute man who had always been hungry dreamed of his favorite dish—noodles and cheese—and craved to eat it, even if only once in his lifetime. He had a dream in which he saw a heaping bowl of noodles standing before him, shining with a topping of butter and cheese. He inhaled the enticing aroma deeply, licked his lips and saw that the bowl before him grew larger and larger, filling his little room, bursting forth into the yard, and covering everything in sight with his beloved noodles. He was standing before this wondrous delicacy and could not take a bite. He had no fork. The next day, before going to sleep, he took a fork with him to bed...." We listened to my father's prolific storytelling even before we read *Shalom Aleichem*.

There were times when we suffered financial hardships, and even hunger. My mother worked hard, and was, in fact, the only breadwinner in our family of seven. She always kept a neat and tidy home and the door was always open to our friends. She nurtured us with love, warmth, and devotion. Life was particularly difficult for her when my father was sick. He had an ulcer and suffered severe attacks during which he worked little and then only with great difficulty. He would sit at his workbench for a few hours until suffering the next attack of pain. He was forced to take frequent breaks from his work. I saw my father suffering and admired his character. The moment the attack passed he returned to his workbench, his good spirits revived, and he continued to work and hum to himself, as if nothing had happened.

Mother worked exceedingly hard, quietly going about her tasks, and no one outside the family knew anything about what went on in our house, or our financial straits. There were years when we each had only one change of clothing. Mother had no time to rest after finishing the housework, and continued working through the night. She would launder and iron our clothes, so we always were well dressed for school, with a few new patches here and there, and we were always meticulously clean.

My mother's stomach began to swell, and for several months she, all of us, and anyone who saw her, were convinced that she was pregnant again. After some time, she began to harbor suspicions. Particularly during the morning hours, when she woke up early, she noticed something strange: she was nauseous, as she had been during her previous pregnancies, but when she was carrying her other five children she had never felt so heavy.

When she could no longer muster the strength to get up, and could barely move at all, she agreed to my father's plea to see a doctor, who, to my parent's surprise, immediately diagnosed a stomach tumor. My mother had silently borne her suffering, and only we, the children, could not hide our concern for her. I was still very young at the time. Mother was hospitalized, and the next day, in an emergency operation, a seven kilogram tumor was removed from her stomach; it weighed more than a baby. The operation was complex, after which Mother was confined to bed for several weeks.

During this period, my brother Eliezer took over at home at the expense of his studies. He was often forced to be absent from school in order to fulfill all his duties. His friends brought him the schoolwork and he worked on it late into the night. He was like a mother to us; he helped us dress, brushed our hair, and did all the household chores until Mother had fully recuperated and was back on her feet.

Once, my brother was on his knees, scrubbing the floorboards with a brush before the Sabbath, and two girls from his class came in. When they saw him they rolled up their sleeves, forcibly took the brush out of his hands, pushed him aside, and told him, "This isn't a man's work."

Eliezer was also in charge of our education. We admired and loved him very much. He continued to guide us even after he completed his matriculation and left home to continue his studies in Prague, from where he wrote us often, recommending books for us to read.

We were avid readers. It was extremely costly to go to the cinema and its antecedent, the silent movie. I can count on the fingers of one hand the number of movies I saw as a young girl. We used to take books out of the library. There were popular books that were passed among our friends, among them the finest classics, such as Tolstoy's *Anna Karenina*, Dostoyevsky's *Crime and Punishment*, Emil Zola's *Germinal*, Nabokov and Feuchtwanger, and many other fine writers, with whom I passed many enjoyable hours. I would become engrossed in my reading and forget about everything that was going on around me

My brother went off to study and we, the younger children, could not understand the meaning of an empty nest. We reminded our mother that we were still at home; it was only Eliezer who was far away. This is what we would say to her when she wrung her hands in sorrow and told us how much she missed our brother.

I was deeply impressed by one of the books on my brother's list, *The White Plague*, by the Czech writer, Karl Capek, a close friend of the president. During one of my brother's visits he told me about a play he had seen at the theater in Prague, which was adapted from this book. My brother described it to me so vividly that while I was listening to him I imagined I could actually see the wondrous Jewish doctor—the only one who had the medication for an incurable and fatal disease. He was willing to give the cure only to one poor patient who could not afford it. The incurable white plague rapidly spread throughout the city and country, reaching the royal court. The palace sent emissaries to the doctor, begging him to come at once and give the king his wonder drug, but the doctor refused and they returned empty-handed. The king's emissaries returned on the morrow, and again begged him to come. They promised him any sum of money he wanted if only he would hasten and save the king. The doctor sent them back to the king, asking them to inform the king of his one and only condition: the king would have to promise to release his entire people from paying taxes without delay. The king agreed. The doctor hastened to the palace where the masses had congregated, weeping before the king, relating their disaster, and begging his help. When they saw the doctor their rage increased. None of them were aware of the condition the doctor had stipulated. They beat him, and in the uproar numerous people were trampled down, among them the doctor. When he was knocked down his briefcase fell with him. The agitated crowd trampled on it, thus destroying the only medication that had the power to cure humanity.

At home we had no running water. We used to draw water from a hand pump that stood in the center of the yard. In the winter months the drops of water would freeze and turn into slippery ice. Drawing a bucket of water involved a great deal of maneuvering. I would walk carefully, step-by-step, slip, and slide backwards. When temperatures outside were freezing, the ground was covered in frost, and matters were even more complicated. The pump's handle would not budge and we had to pour hot water inside to free it. When spring came, the ice melted, and this state of affairs came to an end.

Several water buckets stood on a bench at the entrance to our house. We called it "the water bench." Next to the bucket was a cup that was used to draw water for drinking, cooking, and cleaning the house. On the floor was an aluminum bowl used for dirty water. The fact that we had to carry water in tricky conditions made house cleaning and cooking extremely difficult.

I remember the autumn days, when I would wait for the heavy rains and strong winds to shake the tree branches after which a downpour of nuts would fall to the ground. Chaya and I would quickly bundle up in our coats, go out into the rain and wind, and collect the nuts. We would skip in the rain, joyous with our treasure. Our conscience was clear—we left many more nuts on the ground, which would be sufficient for the landlords as well. They were pleasant Czechs whom we liked very much. We were friendly with them and with their daughter, Vlasta, and son, Volodya. Even if they had seen us collecting the nuts they would have pretended they had not. They were wonderful people. The father was a clerk in the municipality; when he came home from work he would immediately change from his official clothes, take off his necktie, put on an open-necked shirt and shorts, take a hoe or rake in hand, go out into the garden, and toil among his flower beds.

We spent a great deal of time with the Czech children who lived on our street. It was called Rose Street due to the beautiful front gardens with their vibrant roses and other flowers in a wide range of colors. We would play hide-and-seek, and tag, and other games with the Czech children who lived in our neighborhood. My sister Chaya and I would speak in Hebrew and warn one another from our hiding place. They heard us and would call out, "*zehirut, zehirut*" (careful, careful), just like us. We loved to play the "statue" game. We would stand in a circle, one of us was chosen as the "seller," who would then wind up an imaginary handle on our back, and we would turn into a music box and sing: "*Smardalevi Jid…Smardalevi Jid…*" I would sing along with the rest of the children. Only years later I understood the words I had sung: "Dirty Jew, dirty Jew." The Czechs were agreeable, open-minded people, but it seems that the hatred of the Jews that had existed for many generations was embedded deep inside them and expressed in a seemingly innocent children's game.

The privy was at the back of the yard. It was a small wooden hut built of a few planks of wood, abounding with cracks. In the winter it was difficult to do what we had to, but we enjoyed going out there in the late spring and summer. We would sit there even when we did not need to, since to us it was a Garden of Eden. Between the door and the roof there was a large space through which a number of pear tree branches grew. The fruit oozed nectar. I would pick the fruit, and eat it. There was also a large space between the door and the ground, which caused us great suffering in the winter months when the snow and cold penetrated.

During the cold winter months I loved skimming over every frozen puddle. I would slide and feel guilty because I knew that I was wearing out the heels of my shoes, and repairing them was very costly. But I could not control myself. That wonderful feeling of sliding more than compensated for my wrongdoing.

My father told me that during the cold winter days it was extremely dangerous to touch our fingers, or ears, because if they froze they could be severed from our body and remain in our hands. One day a neighbor came in. He stood at the entrance and Father shouted at him not to dare touch his ears. I was frightened and imagined his frozen ears falling off his head and lying in his hands.

I loved the street we lived on, which was far away from the center of town. It was a quiet street, with a tree-lined sidewalk. The plants that climbed the walls made it difficult for the postman to find the house numbers. Across the street from our yard was a vast park filled with ornamental trees, among which were lilac bushes of every color; I loved their intoxicating smell. There were benches among the bushes. Sometimes when I passed by I would take a shortcut home and see a secluded young couple in these beautiful surroundings. The park attracted many hikers. In the middle, among the tall chestnut trees, stood a big building, which housed the government ministries.

The old house had a long history. In the days of the Austro-Hungarian empire it served as a place of recreation for the princes and nobility. It was one of the Kaiser's palaces. It changed "roles" in accordance with the times. After the Hungarians conquered our region, they turned it into torture chambers. We called it the inquisition building. The Hungarian gendarmerie, who used to wear the arrow cross and even surpassed the German swastika-bearers in their cruelty, would take their victims to this building, which stood deep in the big park, and thus the cries of the victims were not heard. Rumors about the building circulated in the city. Everyone knew but no one dared to speak about it for fear of the regime's long and vengeful arm.

In winter, I used to peek through the cracks in the fence of the local skating rink, to watch the happy children skating there. The view was particularly lovely in the evenings when the rink was floodlit. I left the place, knowing that I had to be satisfied with sliding over frozen puddles.

Conditions at home were particularly difficult when my father's ulcer attacks came one after the other, and he could no longer eat. Anything he swallowed only intensified his pain. His condition worsened until he could no longer digest food at all. Left with no other option, my sister Chaya and I would take turns going to the home of a righteous woman, the grandmother of one of my classmates. The elderly lady would give us clear chicken broth every day, and we would fill a pot we had brought and take it home. It was the only thing Father could digest. I felt terrible—I was a child, and stood there like a beggar, asking for alms. I am unable to describe the feeling, but the need to help my father overcame my shame and I continued going to the old woman as long as I had to. When I reached this generous woman's home, I saw, for the first time in my life, what wealthy people's kitchens looked like. The stove was covered in brimming pots of all shapes and sizes, the kind we did not have at home. I would inhale the wonderful smells. At home we used two or three large pots. Mother would cook only one dish in each. One day it would be beans, the next day cabbage, and the following day a combination of beans and cabbage.

When Father's pain was alleviated for a time, he was so happy to feel well again, and we could no longer see the suffering man he once was. He was again in a good mood, returned to his workbench, and began working while humming a tune; or he sang as if nothing had happened. This continued until the next attack. Despite his poor health, Father was the one to decide on how every penny would be spent.

His priorities were different from the usual priorities of poor families. We enjoyed "luxuries" such as a metal bathtub, at a time when there was no running water, while many people were satisfied with bathing once a week at the public baths. We were proud that we had a bathtub at home, as well as a thermometer, which the doctor would usually provide when visiting patients. We bought a Yiddish and Hungarian newspaper every day, and we had a bookshelf to which new books were occasionally added, books we either bought or borrowed from the library.

My father's formal education consisted of three years of study in the *heder* with a rabbi, and four years of elementary school. Nevertheless he was an educated man, attentive to what was going on in the world and left-wing in his convictions. Before the age of television and at a time when even radio was rare in our town, and reached only a few homes, Father would give us information he had gleaned from the newspapers about events in faraway places. An item about a volcano erupting or a coal mine caving in and burying scores of miners became the subject of animated conversation at home.

I well remember one incident from those days. It was a cold winter and our situation was dismal. Representatives of the authorities often paid us a visit demanding that we pay our taxes, which we could not, and each time they threatened to seize our belongings. Their threats were useless since we did not have enough money even for our daily living expenses. The first time the authorities appeared they left our home with a chest of drawers, the next time they took a cabinet or another piece of furniture, until we were left with only our beds and the stove, which they could not take because it was a wall fixture. The only piece of furniture they left was my father's workbench.

The next day the door flew open and three ruffians entered. They went straight to the workbench, next to which Father was seated. They took hold of the bench, as if it already belonged to them. I watched as Father rose, gruffly knocked over his stool, grabbed his jacket, threw it over his shoulders, and said: "If you take my workbench, I have nothing more to do here, take my wife and children and support them, because I am leaving." Father left the house, slamming the door behind him.

It was nearly noon and we, the young children, were in bed, covered in blankets because the room was freezing and bed was the only place we could keep warm. I saw my mother's sad face; she stood wringing her hands, helpless, tears filling her eyes, until she saw the bailiffs leave the house empty-handed. My mother was still standing there, happy that this visit had passed without losing any more possessions, when she heard my father laugh. He came in merrily, and told her how he had succeeded in fooling them this time too, and explained that the reason he hastened to leave with his coat was that in one of its pockets was the money he had received for shoes he had delivered the day before.

We felt an improvement in our financial situation mainly when we moved from a one-room apartment to a slightly larger one. There, next to Father's workbench, the future of my education and that of my brothers and sisters was decided.

The founder of the Hebrew elementary school was Haim Graber, who was my teacher for four years. After concluding elementary school I continued at the Hebrew Gymnasium, whose founder and first principal was Dr. Haim Kugel. He invested all his energy in the field of Hebrew and Zionist education in Munkács and in Carpatorus, revealing his commitment to Jewish, national, human, and Zionist causes. He was elected a member of the Czech parliament in Prague representing the "Jewish Party," and fought for Jewish rights as a proud Jew and Zionist, and won our profound admiration.

His first visit to our home brought a turnabout to our lives. Dr. Kugel sat down next to my father at his workbench, and tried to convince him to agree to send his son, my brother Eliezer, to a Hebrew school, a school that had not yet been founded, but which he planned to establish. My father liked the idea, and he agreed. Father had a positive attitude towards anything that would bring progress. There were other Jews who greeted Dr. Kugel's initiative warmly. Opposition to the Hebrew Gymnasium came from another direction, from the religious community. They heard about this "non-kosher" institution that was to be founded, and claimed that such a thing would never come about. They believed that Divine Providence would intervene on their behalf and would not allow the establishment of a school for "Zionist heretics." When building began in earnest they were surprised to see that the institution was indeed going up brick by brick, and they could not comprehend why God did not tear it down.

The Hebrew Gymnasium did not receive legal permission from the authorities, and Dr. Kugel fought hard against bureaucracy. He was promised a building permit , but somehow it never arrived. Despite all these impediments, building continued with his support. Financing it was not an easy matter. Officially, the authorities did not recognize the institution and did not grant it financial support as it did with other kinds of schools. Despite the hardships, the Gymnasium's influence was felt deeply in the city, and slowly permeated the community. A short time after its establishment, Zionist youth movements from all streams developed in our city and began their activities within the walls of the Gymnasium, after school hours, with the approval of Dr. Kugel, our principal.

Among the students there were religious boys and girls who belonged to the *Mizrahi* movement. Within a short time every youth movement had its own clubhouse. For a while, the *Mizrahi* club was situated in the same building and on the same floor as our *Hashomer Hatzair* club. We used to snigger when we saw them dancing in two circles, one for boys and one for girls. However we maintained good relations with them. Among our guests at home was a religious, well-educated and handsome young man. He liked the atmosphere in our home, which was so different from his own; his parents were religious, he had eleven brothers and sisters who were noisy all hours of the day. He could never find a quiet corner, a place where he could be by himself. When he came to our home he would hide his side locks behind his ears, go into the other room with my sister, and there they would sit, undisturbed, and talk, or read poems together, exchanging views on a poet or writer, things which in his home would be considered "non-kosher."

The youth movements grew and absorbed the finest young people. The objective was two-fold: to provide an appropriate place for students to prepare their homework, since most of the families were large and lived in cramped quarters, and also to use these meetings for discussions, as preparation for future *aliyah* to Palestine and settlement of the land.

As the strength of the Zionist groups grew, quarrels between us students and the fanatical religious youth increased. We had fierce arguments with them that often degenerated into violence and stone-throwing "battles." We would meet at the Gymnasium for activities on Saturdays, and when we left the building the religious youth would attack us, throw stones at us, and chase us, and we retaliated with a vengeance until they retreated.

Dr. Kugel was concerned about the future of his students and wanted to equip graduates with a broad education, both in the humanities and the sciences, so that when the time came to enroll at university, the name of the school would be "The Hebrew Real-Reform Gymnasium of Munkács." The Gymnasium was unique. Relations among students, and between students and teachers, were extremely relaxed, without barriers and devoid of customary formality. It was the only institution where students could relate to their teachers as friends. In other schools, teachers were referred to in the third person, or as "your honor."

Over a long period, in fact until the persecutions began, the two youth movements, *Hashomer Hatzair* and *Dror*, carried on heated arguments. The *Dror* members accused us, members of *Hashomer Hatzair*, of being arrogant, regarding ourselves as the elite, but we were not to blame. It so happened that students joined *Hashomer Hatzair*, while the artisan apprentices and the girls, the majority of whom were seamstresses, joined *Dror*. No one directed the young people to one place or another. This division just happened.

One of the prominent figures in the *Dror* movement was my Gymnasium teacher, Menahem Bergenbaum, who later in Israel changed his surname to Oren. I liked him more than all my other teachers mainly because of the beautiful Hebrew he spoke. When he said my name I heard the sounds of *Eretz Israel*. When he reached Palestine he was what one would call "a realizer," and in order to realize the supreme purpose to which he aspired, he went to live and work at Kibbutz Tel Yosef, where he married one of his students, whom he had loved from the days he was a Gymnasium teacher, and raised a family. He lived an active and creative life, had a happy family, until one fateful day, he was killed in an automobile crash. But at the Gymnasium in Munkács, we shared wonderful and unique experiences with him. At school, he was my teacher, but in the afternoons he would often visit my parents' home and become a member of the family. Only rarely in life does one meet such a person. He was totally devoted to his fellow men, aspired to improve the conditions of the needy, and those of the entire community. This is the way he behaved as a teacher at the Hebrew Gymnasium and as a counselor in the *Dror* youth movement.

After his tragic death, Gymnasium students and city residents attended a commemoration evening. A film about his life was screened, and among other things, it showed him traveling the length and breadth of remote Carpathian towns and villages, bringing the Zionist message to the homes of the Jews there who lived in total destitution among their gentile neighbors.

After the war, together with numerous other illegal immigrants who embarked on the "illegal" ship, we arrived in Cyprus where I remained for over a year, awaiting my turn for *aliyah*. Menahem Oren came to Cyprus as an emissary from Palestine. He was a *Dror* counselor and Hebrew teacher. Our first meeting, after years of separation, was deeply moving. In his presence I unburdened myself of the hardships I had endured up to this point, as I stood at the "threshold of our homeland." We would meet frequently, as we were among the teacher-counselor staff in Cyprus, each of us a member of our respective movements. At the end of the day, after the students had gone to bed, we would walk through the camp, and we often talked until the early hours of the morning.

Another personality from my school days was a teacher by the name of Arieh Sola. He managed to make *aliyah* before the war. He taught Hebrew literature, Bible, and history at a high school in Palestine. I encountered a "problem" with him since he was my brother Eliezer's best friend, and he would frequent our home where he knew he was always welcome. Like my brother, he too regarded my father as a friend with whom he could talk about anything. At school I was embarrassed; I smiled at him when I raised my hand in order to get permission to speak.

He brought Margalit, his girlfriend, on one of his visits to our home, and introduced her. He particularly wanted to hear my father's impressions. She was petite, delicate, and beautiful. He was very much in love with her and was glad to receive my father's blessing. They were married, raised a family, and had children and grandchildren before Arieh took sick and died. His widow, Margalit Sola, lives near us in Netanya, and whenever we are there we visit her. She speaks a great deal about our house. She is older than I am and remembers things about my home that I never knew.

When the Gymnasium's principal asked Arieh to study education and teaching at the university in Prague, he accepted, completed his studies, and returned to us as a literature and history teacher.

Years passed and he retired, but he continued his admirable work. He was a volunteer speaker anywhere he was invited. I too invited him to our kibbutz and was extremely proud of him—my good friend and erstwhile teacher.

As the Hebrew Gymnasium did not receive support from the government institutions, only students who could afford to cover the expensive tuition fees were able to attend. We were not among those who could afford tuition, but despite this we were lucky to be able to study there. The principal, who was well aware of our financial situation, exempted us from tuition fees. He also recommended us as private tutors to parents of children who encountered difficulties in their studies, mainly in the Hebrew language, at which we excelled.

As a fourth-grade student I was proud to be a Hebrew teacher for first-grade students. My wages were meager, but I was very happy with every penny I brought home. I never complained about our financial straits, but there were times when I was compelled to "demonstrate" our distressful situation in class. For example, when students were required to buy school books and equipment, which were very expensive, the teacher would ask those who could not bring the money to raise their hands, and I was always in this group. I was not the only one, but the feeling was very unpleasant.

We were really poor; our only source of income was my father's work as a shoemaker. When we grew up, we, the children, also helped out to the best of our ability. Eliezer was a significant help. While he was a student at the Gymnasium he gave many students private lessons in physics and mathematics.

After matriculating he went to study in Prague. At the request of the Gymnasium's teaching staff he enrolled in the humanities department, so that when he graduated he could join them. However, he lived with two other students and showed great interest in their medicine books. During the second semester he dropped out of the humanities course and moved to the faculty of medicine.

Eliezer was an excellent student and a much sought-after tutor. The payment he received for his teaching covered his expenses, tuition, and even left over some extra that he sent home. It was a substantial monthly sum that paid for wood or coal for heating the house, as well as making up the rent. His students' parents received him well. When he came home once during vacation, he showed us a beautiful wristwatch, an expensive item in those days, and still considered a luxury. It was given to him as a gift by the parents of one of his students.

When he was home I could not control myself, and would open his biology books. I spread out the book cover that opened up like a huge map, on which there was a picture of the male human body, with arrows pointing to the various body parts. I slowly closed the heavy tome, turned it over, and opened the back cover. There too a big picture opened up, this time to reveal a woman's body with all its various parts.

I once saw my father standing with my brother, who had arrived on one of his vacations from Prague. They were both smiling, leaning on the windowsill, and secretively talking, like two friends, watching me. Later I discovered that they were talking about me. My brother, who already saw himself as something of a specialist, "a budding doctor," had asked my father whether I was "grown up" already.

Despite our poverty I have fond memories of holidays at home. We were not religious—on the contrary—but we loved the Jewish tradition and its customs, which we kept. Every Friday night my mother lit the Sabbath candles. When each of us was born, another candlestick was added. My mother stood before them, covered her face with both hands, and said the Sabbath blessing. The two *hallahs* on the white tablecloth were covered with a small cloth on which was embroidered: "And the heaven and the earth were finished and all their host." My father brought a bottle of sacramental wine and wineglasses. The candles heralded a change in atmosphere, but we did not regard them as sacred. We could write by their light or do whatever we pleased, things that were strictly forbidden in religious homes. In our home, we observed only the beautiful aspects of the tradition, the parts of Judaism that we loved. We had our own *Kabbalat Shabbat*. Later, after the meal was concluded, we sang Sabbath songs accompanied by the mandolin, guitar, and other musical instruments.

Before Tu B'Shevat [the New Year for Trees] my mother would buy carob, figs, and raisins, which we loved and ate in reverence because they came from the Land of Israel, or at least that is what we were told. We removed the tiny pits from the carob pods and played "Odds and Evens" (later when I came to Israel I found out that these were used as cattle feed).

I loved the festival of Passover. Before the holiday we completed all the preparations, just like our religious neighbors, and despite the fact that at home we could secretively eat *hametz* [leavened bread], to the outside world we kept the tradition. My mother would collect breadcrumbs on a wooden spoon and add them to the bonfire in which all the *hametz* was burned.

We observed the traditional Seder night, reading from the *Haggadah* [the book of liturgy for the Passover service], filling our wineglasses until the meal, after which Eliezer and Shlomo's friends would arrive, and we would sing and play well into the night. We did not relinquish the *afikoman* [a piece of matzah broken off and hidden from the children, who search for it and are promised presents as a reward for finding it], because in our family, it was only symbolic, as we could not afford expensive presents anyway.

I remember one Purim in particular, when I was still a little girl. I saw my father standing behind the stove, crying—real tears flowing from his eyes. I was frightened and ran to tell my mother, who explained to me that Father was not used to wine, and perhaps he had drunk one glass too many.

I loved school and the Hebrew language; I was a member of a group whose banner was emblazoned with "Jew—speak Hebrew." We would post these banners on the walls of our Gymnasium, along the long corridors and in the classrooms, because many students would forget they knew Hebrew outside the classroom. They spoke Hungarian, German, Czech, or any other language spoken at home. I was among the few who devoutly followed the slogan of the banner, and was proud to disseminate the language.

Our school was a small island of *Eretz Israel* set in the sea of the Diaspora, a lonely island in the heart of the Czechoslovakian Republic, the only Jewish Gymnasium in the entire country. Many Jews from the neighboring towns and villages, as well as from faraway Prague, the capital of the Czech Republic, and from Slovakia, sent their children to study at this unique school, because its aims were progressive and Zionistic—preparation for pioneering and *aliyah* to the Land of Israel.

As a young child I loved to watch the Czech people's colorful parades on their national holiday. They would march in beautiful blue, white, and red costumes, the colors of their flag. I loved everything about the Czechs but I particularly loved their national anthem, which opened with the words: "*Kde domov moy*" [Where is my home], a question I asked myself as well.

I loved the scouts, proud young Czechs who openly demonstrated their self-confidence and love of their homeland. We, the Gymnasium students, always maintained pleasant and friendly relations with them.

We would return from a parade, having walked the length of the town center's promenade, proud Zionists. We sang Hebrew songs aloud, heads held high. The Czech scouts would await us at their meeting place near school. When we returned from a school trip, or from one of our nature outings, or on Lag Ba'Omer [the thirty-third day after the Passover festival], they were always there, receiving us with prolonged applause, wearing festive costumes, their band playing Hebrew songs for us, and our meeting would end in vivacious circles dancing the *Hora* [a traditional Hebrew dance].

I admired the Czechs and their culture, which was so different from those of all the other neighboring countries. We enjoyed living in a democracy as opposed to our neighbors, who suffered under dictatorial regimes.

I also loved the Czech flag and the national costume, until I joined *Hashomer Hatzair*, and from then on I had a national anthem and flag of my own, and a homeland for which I yearned.

At the entrance to every classroom in school there was the "Blue Box," a metal box with the map of *Eretz Israel*. Students would donate money, each according to his or her ability. We would give up buying candy at recess. At the end of the month the boxes were ceremoniously emptied. There was fierce competition between the classes. The class that donated the largest sum would win a prize, to organize the next *Kabbalat Shabbat*, which was considered a great honor.

When I was in fourth or fifth grade I fell in love with one of my classmates. I sat in the last row, directly behind him. His name was Ze'ev Morgenstern; in later years he changed his name to Shahar. I was so much in love with him that I was shy in his company. It was particularly important to me to make a good impression on him. Every time I raised my hand, having to disclose that I did not have the money to pay for something, I would raise my hand no higher than my shoulder, and look at the teacher to see whether he had counted me.

For many years we held an annual Gymnasium reunion, but these became increasingly infrequent. At one of these reunions I sat next to Ze'ev Shahar and revealed my past love: he was surprised and expressed regret that he had not known it at the time.

My years of study were full of happiness. The students and teachers were motivated and inspired by creative projects, and this is how we filled our time. We produced numerous operas and operettas; Vachtel, one of our teachers, reached the conclusion that an outstanding institution such as ours should also produce a Hebrew opera. Since he was the kind of person who took his ideas seriously, he wrote the libretto and melodies, which were an expression of love and endeavor, of building the homeland. From a musical point of view we were familiar mainly with operatic arias, but in our opera the text had a unique function: it expressed our aspirations and yearnings. *"First we build, only the tents, the tents—later we go out to work… and when the grapes ripen, we pick them, we pick them and rejoice in the harvest festival."* These activities took place mainly in elementary school. In the higher classes schoolwork became more and more intensive, but the pioneering spirit prevailed.

Our school accepted only Jewish children, but there was one exceptional case. Margit and Josef Straus, a Christian couple, lived in our city, and showed great interest in our school. Josef was familiar with its unique social atmosphere, and he was captivated by it. He asked the principal to accept his son, and he was indeed accepted as a special case. He was the only non-Jewish child in the school.

A few years later, when persecution of the Jews began, and before the ensuing catastrophe, Josef Straus invited Amos, the son of the Bible teacher, engineer Eliyahu Rubin, to come live with them, although he was well aware of the fact that by taking in a Jewish child, he was endangering his own life. Both fathers could not envision what was about to happen, nor that by this act, Amos, a Jewish boy, would remain safe in the home of a Christian, who had not forgotten the kindness of a Jewish teacher. Amos lived in his house posing as their relative for the entire duration of the war. The Straus family saved the life of one Jewish boy, the only one to survive among thousands of Jewish children who lived in the ghetto before deportation.

In Yad Vashem in Jerusalem, on the first tree along the left of the Avenue of the Righteous Gentiles, hangs a plaque upon which is inscribed "In memory of Margit and Josef Straus."

After the war I was among the first to return to Munkács. There were no old people or children among those who returned. Amos was the only Jewish child who had survived. His parents were deported separately to the death camps, but they were among the lucky ones who survived. They returned home to Munkács and went straight to the Straus's home where they were reunited with their only son. On seeing Amos, their joy knew no bounds.

Rumors of anti-Semitism in Poland reached us but it all seemed far away and we preferred to ignore it. We did not believe that this might happen to us too, until the arrival of a young Jewish man who had managed to cross the border and escape, before being put on a train, whose destination was unknown. He told us in Yiddish about his family and his peaceful life in a Polish village. With dreamy blue eyes and a yearning for what he had lost, he sang a song, which later, upon reflection, seemed to be a memento-warning, which at the time we ignored. He sang in a deep voice: *"Arbeit, arbeit, schneit die sangen—on die kusis hartmann klangen"* [Work, work, harvest the wheat, the echoes of the harvesters can be heard from the scythes]. Today the sounds are silenced; Jews no longer plow there.

He finished his song, sat for a long time, looking at us in silence. Confronted with our indifference he decided to warn us and before leaving, said: "This time listen to me. I don't want to frighten you, but you must leave everything and forget about the things you are preoccupied with. Leave at once! Perhaps you can still save yourselves…"

CHAPTER THREE

Under Hungarian Rule

The young man's prophecy came true, with the trouble beginning in the west. On the day that the Czech Sudetenland was annexed to the Third Reich, Fascist Hungary was also given a "gift." The Germans gave our entire region, once known as Carpathian Russia, to the Hungarians, who had not only capitulated to them but also collaborated with them.

After the relatively comfortable life to which we had become accustomed in the Czechoslovakian Republic, we suddenly found ourselves under foreign rule, a dictatorship, about which we knew nothing. In contrast to the Czechs, the Hungarians had never even heard of democracy and we, the Jews, were the first to suffer the changes from the very first day the Hungarians took over my hometown, Mukachevo.

One of the first edicts handed down by the new regime was to remove the sign bearing the name "The Real Reform Hebrew Gymnasium" and replace it with one that read "The Hungarian Jewish Gymnasium." Had only the sign been different, we could have ignored it, but everything changed. Most of the teachers were new; some of our best teachers had fled across the border in an attempt to save their lives.

Suddenly, the school had a totally different character and wherever I went, I heard Hungarian: in the school corridors, the playground, and in the street. The atmosphere changed radically and I couldn't accept the new decrees in my school that I loved so much. How could I change my character in one fell swoop? I loved Hebrew with my very soul and there was no way I could adapt to the new teaching language, Hungarian.

My sisters and I, and many others like us for whom fulfilling the aims of Zionism was a supreme value, left school. I still had to complete two years of study in order to attain my matriculation certificate but I gave it up, while those for whom the certificate was their ideal stayed on.

With the assistance of the Germans, the Hungarians organized themselves very quickly. After only a few days they came to our door. My brother Shlomo was handed a mobilization order but, unlike the non-Jewish boys, he was not given a uniform. In the Hungarians' view, Jews were unworthy of wearing His Highness the Fascist dictator Horthy's uniform on their "contemptible" bodies. They recruited the Jewish boys as laborers, auxiliary personnel in the Hungarian forces—they became the servants of the army.

The day that the Hungarian gendarmes came to our house and took Shlomo away was the last time we saw him. We waited for news of him, fearful of his fate, but he never came home on leave and never wrote. No one ever saw him and no one could tell us where he was or what had become of him.

(For almost fifty years since Shlomo's disappearance, my brother Eliezer continued searching for him by all possible means, seeking to obtain any information about him with which he might be able to trace him. To this end he invested all his time and energy and was helped by friends in Prague from the days he lived there, but we still had no news of Shlomo. Eliezer has a postcard he received from Shlomo that was sent from Prague by a Palestinian Jew he had met there, on which he had written the date, June 28, 1945, and how happy he was to be finally on his way to fulfilling his life's dream. He was going to Russia by train and intended to break his journey at Mukachevo to see whether anyone of our family or his friends was still there. Eliezer did not accept for a moment the possibility I raised of Shlomo not wanting to go to Palestine, for health or ideological reasons, and preferring to vanish from our lives.)

The new regime was a cause of great concern for us. To put it mildly, we didn't like the Hungarians from the moment we were forced under their rule, and not only because of the cultural differences between them and the Czechs. Each day we felt that instead of moving forward and developing, we were in retreat, moving towards an obsolete regime, one more suited to the previous century. Before the aggressors took over, we loved walking around the town streets in our free time—it was something we took for granted— and then suddenly we found ourselves living in a new world, having to observe new customs and restrictions. We used to walk a lot, private cars being a rare commodity, and we rode a great deal on our bikes.

One day I was out walking on the promenade with some of my friends and as we approached the bridge, that only yesterday we were able to cross freely, we found ourselves face to face with a soldier standing guard. An armed Hungarian soldier? We didn't understand exactly what he was guarding or against whom. As far back as my early childhood the bridge had been open for crossing to the other side of the river where we would walk in the green woods or along the winding path that ran up the side of the mountain to the monastery at the top. We couldn't grasp the sudden change. We took one look at the guards and, without a word, we fled. Next day we went out of town in a different direction, towards the brick factory, and there too we could see the armed guards from quite a way off and a similar sight awaited us on our way to the old fortress on the hill. Even before we got off the paved road and onto the dirt path that led to the fortress, there too we could see armed guards. We couldn't understand why there was a need to place guards in the town.

A few of my teenage friends and I decided on a ruse; we just felt like provoking the guards, as we already knew some of their limitations. We walked towards the armed Hungarian soldiers, self-assured, heads held high, relying on the fact that we did not look Jewish. One of my friends said something in Czech to one of them and he shook his head and said, "*Nem ertem*" [I don't understand]. Another asked him, this time in Russian, how to get to a certain street and this too was met with "I don't understand." Then we asked him in English, Yiddish, Hebrew—all the languages we spoke—but our questions received the same reply. We gave him a friendly smile, but perhaps this annoyed him because he lost his patience and his anger boiled over, his faced became mottled, he ground his teeth, and spat angrily, saying, "What kind of people are you who can't even speak Hungarian?" and then cursed us roundly.

With the political changes came a deterioration in the town's economic situation, with the first victims being the Jews, of course. Some of the well-established businessmen still managed to continue their business dealings by fooling the authorities. They used the cover of Hungarian "ownership," while others changed the names on their signs to names with an Aryan ring so as not to endanger their businesses. Jews like us, who just managed to scrape together a living, were the first to feel the effects of the occupation.

For the first time in my life I went out to work to earn money for my family. I was offered a job looking after two young children, aged four and six, the sons of a wealthy Jewish family. So far, this family had not been affected by the new regime's edicts, while I had my first opportunity to see how wealthy people actually lived. They lived in a big, two-story house on the main street, the "Korso" or promenade. On the ground floor was a large store with windows displaying sets of china, glass, and porcelain—expensive merchandise, most of which was imported. They owned other stores that were located next to their own—these they rented at high rates. Their spacious apartment was on the second floor.

My job was to look after the children and play with them while the parents were not at home. When I arrived I immediately introduced myself to the household help—to the servant and the cook. I played with the children and sang to them until lunchtime, when we moved into a corner of the big dining room where the cook served lunch to the children and me. It was the first time I had ever eaten such a meal. After the cook had finished serving the various courses, she sat down with the help in the kitchen where they had their meal. This social separation shocked me, and in my naivete I asked them to join us. They were astonished that I had even asked since it was obvious to them that they could not sit at a table with their employer's children.

I went into my "masters'" bedroom to get something. It was a splendid room with an expensive clayware stove that rose to the ceiling, and by its door, through which the coal was fed, on the parquetry floor, were signs of the night's lovemaking. I was aghast at this disparaging attitude towards the household staff and I was filled with disgust as I felt the depth of the household help's humiliation. After the experience of eating separately from the household staff, and after what I saw in the bedroom, I waited impatiently for the end of the month and once I was paid, I left.

Under the new regime all Zionist activities were prohibited and the Zionist movements were forced underground. The eyes of the law were everywhere and two or three people together was considered unlawful assembly, the people summarily dispersed or arrested. The members of *Hashomer Hatzair* met in secret. The newer members met at people's homes while the older members usually gathered at our house.

We were tense. Each day brought something new and we had no idea what it was to be. But one thing was clear—we had to find the way and move forward, and it was then that we decided to change direction, especially because we were being watched. Our philosophy was the creation of a new Man, one who worked and lived by the sweat of his brow, and this was how we could continue under the close scrutiny of the authorities. The movement established training centers in the guise of farms and thus we continued to adhere to our principal aim, preparation for *aliyah* to Palestine.

Like my friends, I left my home and family and with my sister Chaya traveled to Budapest in order to spread the Zionistic message of our movement. Hungarian Jewry was not an organized community, and there were a great many assimilated Jews among them, and very few knew any Hebrew. Even those who prayed every day only knew the prayers by rote or read them from a transliterated text. They were amazed to hear Chaya and me speaking Hebrew, which for us was perfectly natural. They had never heard fluent Hebrew conversation and at their request we put on a "show"—we simply stood there speaking Hebrew. It all seemed a bit ridiculous to us, but they were astonished by what they heard.

Meanwhile I said goodbye to Chaya when I left for a training farm located near a small town south of Budapest. Our members worked in our truck farm or at neighboring farms while I was appointed cook and thus stayed in the house. I was no stranger to cooking, having cooked at home to help my mother. I accepted the challenge and did my best to prepare good meals with the few provisions we had.

I have two memories of my time at the training farm, one painful and the other amusing. The painful memory is of my first, unrequited love. In retrospect it seems so innocent. I was never short of friends, and at the farm I had a good friend with whom I spent many happy hours. But Pinchas, unlike my previous boyfriends, was not satisfied with our relationship. We liked to be alone in a quiet corner surrounded by bushes, or on the riverbank or a park bench with a book. We would hug and kiss, but nothing more.

I loved Pinchas, whose nickname was "Pinkaleh." Conditions at the farm and the circumstances of our new life did not enable us to spend a lot of time alone. We would lay side by side under the star-studded sky, cover ourselves with a blanket, snuggling together as closely as possible, caressing and kissing. I was in love and I was happy. But from day to day I could see that my boyfriend was not satisfied with what we had. He pressured me to have sex, but I was not yet mentally prepared for it. Aside from that, I thought of him more as a good friend and less as a life partner.

Perhaps it was fate that intervened and put an end to our love. We parted as friends and some six months after I left the farm I was informed of his tragic death in a road accident. He was my first love.

Anyone else would find my second memory amusing, but for me it was more tragic than comic. At the time, the National Zionist Congress was being held in Budapest and, together with two other people, I was elected as a delegate of the training farm. We reached Budapest, and found the old building—which was one of many such impressive buildings in the Hungarian capital—in which the Congress was being held. Budapest is very similar to Vienna, although it suffered great neglect under the Communist regime, so today not much remains of the splendor of the Austro-Hungarian Empire. We went inside, climbing a broad, thickly carpeted staircase that muffled the sound of our footsteps, to the second floor. On the landing of each floor the wall was covered by a huge mirror.

We reached the landing leading to the next floor and in the mirror I saw a young girl and two young men linking her arms. The girl seemed somehow familiar. We continued up the stairs to the next landing where I saw the same sight, two young men in white shirts—obligatory for the Congress—and dark trousers, and the young woman also in a white blouse and wearing a fashionable pleated skirt, and then I saw in the mirror how the pleats around her hips had opened. It was then that I realized that the skirt did not quite fit… We climbed to the next floor, where again I saw my reflection in the mirror—and couldn't believe my eyes! Another floor, and there was no doubt that the young girl was none other than me. I was stunned! I remember that throughout the ceremony, the speeches by the VIPs, and the singing of the anthems while my hand was raised in the *Hashomer Hatzair* salute, I could think of only one thing: how had I reached such impossible proportions?

Since my childhood I had never been slim and always had a slightly full figure. How had it happened, I thought to myself, and immediately realized who, or rather what, was to blame.

At the farm I used to cook and everyone smacked their lips in satisfaction, but I never sampled my own wares. I sometimes tasted my dishes, but no more. My daily fare was crispy crackling sandwiched between slices of fresh white bread, a real delicacy of fried pork rind, the like of which I had never tasted before. That was my breakfast, lunch, and supper.

Life at the farm was very modest and simple and we didn't even have a real mirror, only a small shard that the boys used for shaving. I remained alone in the house and inspected myself in the splinter of a mirror, seeing only my facial features and nothing else, while here in Budapest I could see myself for the first time in all my huge glory. My God, I thought, what have I come to! And all because of my love for white bread and crackling.

Due to my father's deteriorating health I returned home and continued looking for work, as Mother was our sole breadwinner. After a long period of searching I finally found a job that seemed to be tailor-made for me. First and foremost it had the tremendous advantage of my being able to do it at home without neglecting my duties, as the eldest daughter, of looking after Father. Not only that, I also enjoyed the new work very much, as it gave me a chance to be truly creative.

That winter, a new knitwear fashion that had taken the world by storm reached us from Norway and Sweden—highly decorative work known as "Swedish knitwear." One day, as I passed the window of a wool shop that employed a large number of knitters, I saw a garment that caught my eye. It was beautifully knitted, quite distinctive, and original, and on display it served its purpose by attracting the interest of passers-by who then went into the shop and bought more wool.

I went inside and suggested that I knit them a garment for sale. I took the saleslady outside and showed her the sweater with the special design and promised to knit a similar one for her. She gave me the wool and I worked on the sweater in every spare moment I had, and a few days later I took them my first effort. They were unable to conceal their amazement and on the spot gave me some more wool together with a promise to employ me on a permanent basis.

In the evening, when I had finished my housework, I used to sit at the table by the light of the oil lamp and draw designs on squared paper. Then I would count the stitches on an angora garment so that I could see how the black wool brought out my beautiful designs, such as a dove carrying a stamped envelope in its beak. On another I knitted the head of a reindeer with huge antlers, and each garment I knitted was an original one-of-a-kind.

My work was tremendously successful and I found it difficult to keep up with the orders. The owner of the wool shop gave the simpler work of the back and sleeves to the other knitters so that I could keep up with the demand for my designs. By the standards of those days, my wages were high since people were prepared to pay a lot of money for an original knitted garment, but only a small percentage came to me—most of the money went to the owner.

Then, quite suddenly, and thanks to a recommendation of one of my teachers, I was offered a wonderful job. In the meantime, my father's health had improved considerably so that I was able to accept the offer and leave home for the time being. Although the work seemed to be eminently suitable, I still had some reservations about leaving my home and family. I traveled south to a country town, to a highly respectable Hungarian family of assimilated Jews. Only the new regime reminded them of their faith, and compelled them to remember who they were and what awaited them.

In the wake of the anxiety felt by the Jews came concern for themselves and especially their children. They felt the noose tightening around their necks and saw the bleak future, and they wanted to be ready to leave the country when the time came. They had been looking for a Hebrew teacher for quite a while and when I was recommended they invited me to come to their home and live with them, teach them and their children Hebrew, and spend the days with their two sons, aged eight and ten. What they wanted most of all was that I speak only Hebrew. After school, when I told the children stories about *Eretz Israel*, we were joined by the parents who displayed a keen interest in what was happening in Palestine, a country about which they knew nothing and had never heard of before.

In retrospect, this was one of the happiest periods of my life. The couple were amiable and educated, and they took me into their family and made me feel wanted. One day they bought me a bicycle so that I could join the boys for their daily ride. They also invited me to join them on all their visits to family and friends and I was part of all their trips with the boys.

I loved going out riding with the boys when we were joined by their private math teacher, who also kept an eye on us. He came to the house every day to teach them, and their parents were extremely satisfied with their progress. This was the beginning of a wonderful friendship between the teacher and me. The boys would pump their bike pedals in front of us and we would ride behind. Time after time, our eyes would meet, and our talks continued in the evenings, when just the two of us went out together. Although I had had a few suitors before him, he was different and I hoped that, like me, he was unattached. He had my trust from the first moment, our relationship was beautiful and sincere, our closeness was mutual and modest, which was characteristic of relationships at the time. Our friendship became stronger, I liked him, and I could sense his feelings for me, and in the evenings it was hard for us to say goodnight after standing together kissing and hugging for a long time. We began talking about our future and then, without warning, our relationship came to an end.

I received a letter from home with news that my father was very ill, and Mother asked me to come home immediately because his condition was deteriorating. Eliezer had taken Father to Prague, where he was examined by a specialist who might have been able to alleviate his suffering. But he had returned without a cure for his ulcer. I spent many hours at his bedside and it was then he taught me how to play chess. I sometimes sat there for over an hour, hoping that he would feel better, and then we would take out the chessboard. He was impossible to beat and was proud of his every victory.

Our hardships at home continued because of Father's illness. One day my parents decided that there was no alternative but for my mother to go and work as a cleaner at a famous spa hotel in Carlsbad, Czechoslovakia, where she would be assured a good wage. Mother accepted the offer of work, left home, and her family that was so concerned for her, and went off to Carlsbad. The spa hotel was very well known from the days of visiting royalty, and up to that time some very wealthy people frequented the place for what we call today "a bit on the side"—far from home, wives, and husbands. Mother was a very good-looking woman, with her ready smile and blue eyes, and because she did her job assiduously she became a favorite of the manager and the rest of the staff after a very short time. The wealthy guests, too, would look at her appreciatively and say a few complimentary words to her, which she liked to hear. But there were also hotel guests who she considered repulsive. They would wait for her in the other room or behind the door, grab her, and start hugging and kissing her. Most of them were fat and flushed with drink, and this was even more revolting for her. Mother did not dare refuse them because one complaint about her would have meant dismissal.

She suffered in silence for several months and cried at night until she decided she could stand it no longer. She wrote to Father telling him everything, describing her suffering in great detail. Father read the letter, seething with anger. My mother's situation worried him; he loved her and felt that he had to do something to help her, to intervene, but he didn't know how. He told a good friend of his, a printing worker at one of the daily papers, about Mother's letter.

In those days printing was still done using the old methods of typesetting. Father's friend agreed to help him. In one edition of the paper, he put in a small insert that read: "X is very sick and on his deathbed. If his wife reads this, she should come home as quickly as possible."

Mother, who knew Father better than anyone, smiled happily and took the paper to the hotel manager and showed him the insert with a look of deep sadness on her face. The manager offered her his sympathy, asked her into his office, and paid her the wages due to her even though she was in breach of her contract. He even added a bonus for her loyal and devoted service. Mother was so happy to be at home with her family once more.

Father organized a kind of chess marathon in our town. One Saturday, some of the town's best players came to our house where Father faced them one after the other, playing non-stop, and beat them all. There he sat, brow furrowed in concentration, not eating or drinking, engrossed in the games. In the evening, after the last of the contestants had left, Father felt unwell and went to bed. Mother went to him and found him burning up with fever, delirious, rambling, and moving imaginary chessmen on an imaginary board. We stood around his bed, watching him with deep concern, especially Mother, who constantly wiped his burning forehead with a damp cloth. But nothing helped and finally we decided to call the doctor. The doctor examined him and soothed our fears, telling Mother that he had chess fever and after a good night's sleep he would wake up a new man.

Gastric ulcers were considered incurable, and Father's trip to Prague with Eliezer had not been successful. Our family doctor referred him to the hospital. The doctors there decided that Father needed an operation, but as the hospital did not have a surgeon who could do the procedure, they suggested that he go to the hospital in the neighboring town, Berehovo, which the Hungarians called Beregsaz. We accompanied Mother and Father to the hospital where we waited for a few days as they kept postponing the operation, until one very cold winter morning, they finally took him into the operating theater. We waited outside during the operation, which took many hours, and when they finally brought Father back, we sat by his bedside, waiting for him to come out of the anesthesia. He opened his eyes for a second but closed them immediately, and we continued to wait.

Most of the time he lay there with a wan smile on his face. I moved closer to him because his voice was weak and he spoke into my ear. He said that now, after the operation, he was the happiest man alive. An end had finally been put to the attacks that had made his life a misery. He spoke slowly, breathing heavily, his head filled with plans for things he had wanted to do in the past but was unable, but now he would recuperate and do as he liked as soon as he got out of hospital.

Mother and I took turns at his bedside. When Mother needed a rest, I sat there, and when she returned I dozed on a bench outside. On the third day after the operation I went to see the doctor and asked about Father's condition and I was very happy to hear his encouraging reply. Today, he said, is the third and critical day after the operation, and if he comes through it with no problems, then the operation will be a success. Mother calmed down a little when I gave her the news and went to have a rest, while I waited until the doctors finished their rounds, and sat down next to Father. He opened his eyes for a second but the most of the time they were closed and the blanket covering him rose and fell with his breathing that suddenly sounded unusually heavy. I looked at him and began to tremble.

He raised his hand slightly, indicating that I should open the window. I couldn't understand why because the room was only slightly heated and it was cold, but I stood on a chair and opened the upper window. A cold breeze wafted in but Father still complained that there wasn't enough air in the room and he couldn't breathe. I rushed to find a nurse and told her what was happening; she went into the room and immediately left to bring another nurse and a doctor. I didn't know what was happening but I realized that his condition was not good. All the activity around Father's bed frightened me; the ward sister asked me to wait outside. I was stunned and confused, all our beautiful hopes had been dashed and I was very worried. I waited outside, trembling.

The doctor came out, put his arm around me, and told me to hasten to my father while I could still say goodbye to him. Frightening rasping sounds were coming from Father's throat and his eyes were tightly closed. I wept, my body shaking, not knowing what to do. I was frightened, standing alone by Father's bed, knowing that these were my last moments with him, moments in which I didn't know what to do, moments that are burned into my brain, moments I have seen in my mind's eye over the years—as I slept, in my waking hours, missing him terribly.

The time I waited for my mother seemed like eternity. I could only think of one thing: what I would tell her, how I could break the terrible news. When she arrived and saw me, she hurried to Father's room, but they wouldn't let her in. Father was gone. Mother took me in her arms and we wept together and I could feel her heart beating and her tears on my face. She was very angry with herself and was inconsolable because she had listened to the doctors who had soothed her with their optimistic assurances. She had left Father and gone to rest a while, and now, on her return, he was dead. The doctors told her that they had indeed been optimistic and that the operation had been successful, but Father's heart had been unable to stand the strain.

Our meager finances did not allow us to bring Father's coffin home and he was buried in the foreign town in which he had undergone the operation. The funeral was dismal. Only Mother and we three girls accompanied Father on his last journey in that strange town where we didn't know a soul. I remember the pathway in the cemetery, so much so that perhaps I could find it even today. My memory of the route to the cemetery in that strange town is blurry, but apart from that I don't remember a thing—neither the coffin nor the burial ceremony. They have descended into oblivion.

We returned home with a different mother. Her once-smiling face was downcast and there was a deep sadness in her eyes. She tied a black scarf around her head as a symbol of mourning and this added to her bleak appearance that was so different from what we had known in the past. Coming home without Father was very, very hard for us all.

Eliezer had left home long ago and the Hungarians had taken Shlomo for forced labor, we knew not where. Now there was only Mother and her three daughters, and the house seemed so empty without Father. The corner, in the big room that we called the "parlor," was now empty, the corner in which his bed had been placed, so that he could see what was going on in the house. Mother, who had suffered so much in her life, withdrew into herself, bearing her sadness in silence, just as she had during the long, hard years of Father's illness. We girls decided to pamper her as much as we could. We hugged and kissed her at every opportunity and as our financial situation allowed us some small luxuries, we would occasionally surprise her with cakes from the confectionery shop. We loved Mother's baking, an indulgence which we allowed ourselves only on the Sabbath and festivals. She mostly baked yeast cakes made with very few ingredients, and although simple, they were very tasty—but not of the standard of those we bought for her at the confectionary shop.

Less than a year after Father's death, national and nationalist problems arose all around us. In a very short time, the regime in our region, Carpatorus, changed. We were Ukrainians and one day there was unrest following some shots that no one knew who had fired or why. For safety's sake we erected a "barricade" in the house by moving the table under the window, and on it we placed an iron bedstead and other heavy furniture. But we heard no more shooting. As the regime changed, so did the currency, until the Hungarians came and remained in power.

We began to hear rumors of what was happening in the neighboring countries. There was talk of Jews being thrown out of their homes but no one believed it could happen to us. There were those who said that the absence of menfolk, who had been called up to the war, meant that the towns, and especially the farms, were suffering from a shortage of workers, and they reached the conclusion that we might well be sent to work in one of the towns.

On March 20, 1944, the first of Adolf Hitler's troops reached our region. The first decree obliged all the Jews to wear the Yellow Star on their clothing, which made it easier for the Germans to identify a Jew. As I walked down the street each day I witnessed the arbitrary torture and humiliation of Jews.

Everything we had heard about the Germans' attitude towards the Jews, and which we didn't believe could happen to us, now became stark reality.

Everywhere the Germans reached, their first actions were of unbelievable cruelty. The first victims were those whose Jewishness was particularly noticeable. They were attacked viciously, the Nazis pulling the *yeshiva* students' side-locks and tearing the beards from the faces of Jewish men.

It was now clear beyond doubt that something terrible was about to take place. The situation deteriorated from day to day and we knew it could only get worse. We began to think that we would soon be evicted from our home and deported, as rumor had it, like the Jews of Poland and Slovakia.

There was just the four of us, frightened and anxious, for no one knew what tomorrow might bring.

My parents and their five children, 1934

In the Ghetto, 1944

CHAPTER FOUR

In the Ghetto

From this point on, events moved rapidly. The Jews' property and shops were confiscated. Once store owners and tradesmen, Jews now had no work and were confined to the four walls of their homes.

We had been suffering under the Nazi regime for a month, which seemed like an eternity, before we were delivered the second blow, which was even more severe than the first. An order was issued for all Jews to be concentrated in a ghetto. In our town the Jews were scattered; the Nazis established two ghettos for us.

One ghetto was situated on "The Street of the Jews," which, as its name suggests, was populated mainly by Jews, as were the adjacent streets. This was actually the heart of Jewish life, where the synagogues, seminaries, *mikvah*s, and all the Jewish institutions were to be found.

The other ghetto was established on a main street on the other side of town. The Germans fenced and sealed the area; no one was allowed in or out. Our house and yard were within the boundaries of the second ghetto.

From the moment the Zionist movements were forced underground, all the meetings were conducted in our house. Similarly, all the community's representatives or young people who fled from the authorities' persecution were sent to us. We had an open house thanks to Mother, who welcomed everyone with love as if they were her own children.

This continued even after we were concentrated within the ghetto walls. One day Efra Agmon arrived at our house. He was very active in the Jewish resistance movement in Budapest, and since he was using a false identity—masquerading as a high-ranking Hungarian officer—he could move freely. His job was to provide the Jews who were imprisoned in the ghetto with food, money, and "Aryan" papers with which they hoped to escape.

The Hungarian law officers charged him with these offences, putting him on the "Arrow Cross" wanted list. These were Hungarian fascists who resembled the Nazi Germans, but at that time they had not yet surpassed the Nazis' cruelty.

While searching for him they came to our house. Fortunately there was an attic above our apartment that we shared with our next-door neighbors. While the policemen searched our house, Efra hid in the attic above our neighbors' apartment, and when they left and entered the neighbors' apartment, he hid in the attic above ours. He climbed up a ladder that was in the pantry near the kitchen, and he managed to escape them.

Efra told us about an encounter he had had in Budapest. As always, he was dressed in his Arrow Cross uniform, his chest decorated with medals of honor; and as usual, he was in a hurry, when he was suddenly stopped by a young Gentile boy who said: "I know you." He followed him and added: "Yes, I know you are not a Nazi, and certainly not an officer. You are a dirty Jew, once you lived in our neighborhood, and I know you're a Jew." Rudely, the boy swung Efra around, jabbed his gun into his back, and gleefully pushed him forward thinking he would soon hand him over to the enemy. They stopped at the corner and the boy handed Efra over to two young men wearing the same uniform as Efra.

The two praised the boy profusely, telling him that he had done an exceedingly patriotic deed by handing Efra over to them, and that they knew what to do with the "dirty Jew."

The moment the young boy left all three burst out in unrestrained laughter. The two were Efra's best friends, and like him were masquerading in Arrow Cross uniforms.

From the day the ghetto was established in our town, all the families who, like us, were living within the ghetto compound, absorbed many of the Jews who were left outside. Four more families joined us in our cramped apartment. In anticipation of their arrival we removed the closet doors, took out all our bedding and tablecloths since we knew we would not be using them, and threw everything into a pile in the yard. We removed the drawers and shelves from the closets and filled them with the newcomers' suitcases and bags. They brought the bare necessities—one suitcase per adult and one small bag per child. All the floors in the house were covered with mattresses, crowded one next to the other, on which we slept.

The future seemed uncertain; we never knew what we would wake up to the next day, but we all sensed that disaster was becoming more and more tangible. Every family prepared a little food and a change of clothing for the journey. We were ready, although we did not know what for. The house was quiet; even the children somehow knew that this was not the right time for fighting, crying, or hitting one another.

Five mothers labored together over our stove, preparing food for twenty people. All that time we still believed that if they took us out of the ghetto to another place, it would probably be somewhere where we would work in some capacity. One of the rumors had it that they were planning to take us to southern Hungary to work in the fields. Spring somewhat improved the crowded and distressful conditions inside the house.

Among those who lived with us in the ghetto was Naomi, my sister Chaya's best friend, and her family. The two girls had a marvelous and rare friendship. Naomi's family and ours were very different. We came from a simple, almost poor home, which was Zionist and progressive, while she came from an affluent and religious family, which observed the precepts of Judaism. Naomi used to come to see us almost daily. At times she would stay overnight, sleeping with Chaya in the same bed, and often Chaya was invited to sleep over at Naomi's home. Naomi knew that we all loved her.

Her parents were extremely wealthy. They had a great deal of property including a big store with a display window filled with expensive and mainly imported furs. The shop was situated in an exclusive area in the center of town. Her father employed non-Jewish store guards on a permanent basis. He was a good-hearted, pious man, and he paid them generously. He would give them and their families gifts especially before the Christian holidays.

I do not remember much about life in the ghetto, but there was one ray of light—my good friend Chaya. She lived in the "Jewish" street and came with her family to our street, which was situated within the boundaries of the ghetto. They lived a few houses away from us, but all the yards were extremely overgrown and unkempt, and during those hard times, it seemed as if they were all joined together, making up one huge yard. The fences between the yards were low, and almost all their wooden slats were broken.

My friend Chaya had a wonderful voice. She would lean against the fence, raise her eyes to the sky, dreaming she was in another place, and sing Yiddish and Hungarian songs, and songs in all the other languages she knew. With her divine voice she would sing sad and moving songs, and for a short time would make us forget the hardships of the ghetto. (My friend

Chaya survived the horrors of the war, raised a family in Israel, and lived in Kibbutz Ein Dor. However, she returned weak and fragile from the war, was constantly ill, and died young.)

The ghetto was extremely crowded both inside and out. One could not find a quiet place to be alone.

Behind all the apartments, at the end of the yard, there was a row of storehouses; each tenant had a private storehouse. Near the storehouse there was a square pile of logs, laid in criss-crossed layers, which awaited the lumbermen who would come in winter. At times I would escape there. I would climb to the top of the pile, or push myself into the space between the logs. There I would find myself a little corner, far from everyone else, a spot that was mine alone, and for a short while I would forget everything that was happening around me, and spend time with the heroes of Margaret Mitchell's *Gone With the Wind*. I would wonder whether the suffering we endured might someday come to an end like a passing wind. Who knew? When would that wind reach us, and where would it come from?

One spring morning in the ghetto, my mother, sisters, and I went down the steps into the cellar. Mother was holding a long tube, which she had filled with the few pieces of jewelry she still had from her wedding. She put coins and bills into the tube, looked at us, her daughters, and removed the earrings I loved so much—they had a clover-shaped gilded filigree with a green emerald in their center that enhanced her beauty and accentuated her blue eyes. She dug a small hole in the ground with a spade. Each of us dug a bit of earth and removed it. When the hole seemed deep enough my mother took the tube, wrapped it in numerous layers of cloth, placed it in the earth, and we all joined in to cover the hole.

We stood on top of it and tamped down the soil with our feet to conceal any signs of our digging. My mother embraced each of us, held us close to her, and tearfully said: "This is so you, my dear daughters, will have something to start with when you return." That moment made a deep impression on me. Her words were so intense and fateful that at times it seems to me that I am back there again, and can still hear my dear mother saying those words in her sweet voice. The memory of that moment influenced me to title this book "Earrings in the Celler."

Another evening, when the moon was full, the three of us, my sister Chaya, our friend Naomi, and I, rose quietly one after the other from the mattresses we were crowded on, and stood at the window. We had a double set of windows, as was customary in old houses in Europe, as a protection against the harsh winter weather. Between the two windows there was a wide windowsill, on which we rested our elbows. We huddled together, three teenage girls, our hearts full of dreams and romance, breathing in the scents of spring.

It was the beginning of April. The twentieth marked exactly one month since we had been confined to the ghetto. We stood there silently, close to one another, looking up at the moon in the sky. I wondered from where I might see the moon on the following evening, or whether I would ever see it again?

We could hear the sleeping people breathing behind us, and between the snoring we could hear from time to time the quiet sobbing of a child who couldn't fall asleep. We stood silently for a long while, each of us deep in thought, immersed in our feelings. We were exhausted but did not want to give up that wonderful spring night. It was as if we knew then that it was our last one at home. And then a figure emerged from the darkness, passed through the gate, and approached us. When he saw us he suddenly turned on his heel, and began moving away from us. Naomi recognized him and called him to come back, telling him he had nothing to fear and that we were her good friends, just like sisters, and that we had no secrets between us. When he returned, Naomi removed a gold watch from her wrist, handed it to him, and encouraged him to speak openly to the three of us.

He was one of the guards who worked in her family's furrier store. He came closer, stood silently, and looked at us. He did not know where to begin; we saw how hesitant he was, not knowing how to say what he had to say without distressing us. Finally he said that things were not yet clear, and he too did not know what was going to happen, nor did he understand why, but he and all the other policemen had been given orders to report the next morning at dawn, at 3:45 precisely, at the market square. He said this and disappeared into the darkness. We had no time to ask him anything.

We were stunned. For a while we remained silent and confused. We did not know what to do, whether or not to wake up the grownups and share this information with them. In the end we decided to let our families sleep for a few more hours. Who knows where we would all be the following night, and when we would be able to sleep in a bed once again. I doubted whether I would be able to fall asleep, but I was exhausted, was not even able to think; I huddled between my sisters, trying at least to rest a bit, and evidently fell asleep.

"*Heraus, schnell, verfluchte Juden!*" [Out! Quick! Damned Jews!]. The whip hissed, thrashing the air, falling on our shoulders and heads, beating us out of our homes; we stumbled down the two staircases, each of us carrying a bundle or suitcase. The four of us, my mother, my sisters, and myself, looked at one another, trembling, holding hands, and keeping together at all times. The whipping and beating that drove us forward prevented me from taking one last look at our home, the house in which I left all my past, my childhood, my youth, and my entire life.

Now we were a small family. Just the four of us, holding hands in order to stay together. We immediately took on a fifth member, one of our neighbor's daughters, to make up a rank of five; this was what we were ordered to do. We walked slowly, or were rather pushed ahead, accompanied by shouting, curses, and beating. Many could not suffer any longer, and remained on the roadside. The Germans were beating them so badly that we were unable to stop and go over to help them. This is how we walked until we reached the market square, which was by then crowded with frightened people, mothers clutching their babies, men and women, children and old people. The Germans shouted at us and lashed us with their whips, all the time barking at us to keep in ranks of five, followed by an order to sit down on the ground. From that moment on we no longer had names—they counted us like cattle.

The light of dawn revealed the catastrophe in the marketplace. Words cannot describe the sight that has never been erased from my memory. I relive it even now as I write about it. The Germans passed between us, roughly tearing off gold rings from our fingers, chains from our necks, brusquely searching our clothing and bodies for jewelry. They took any money they found, shouting and cursing "*verfluchte Juden*" [damned Jews], and beat us.

The four of us sat together in silence. I saw blood on the faces of those who tried to resist them, and became very frightened. Then we heard a shot, the first one, which was a forewarning. After we heard it everyone began to tremble in fear and no one tried to resist the Germans any further. We sat crowded together on the wet, muddy, and filthy cobblestones of the marketplace; I did not know where to look so as not to see the bloody faces and bodies that surrounded me. Once more the shouting echoed in my ears, and I heard the orders directing us to get up and form ranks of five, and get ready to move. From that moment on and until I escaped the death march, everything was conducted in ranks of five.

We set off. This was to be the last time I walked through the streets of my hometown. The new owners, the Gentiles, who had taken over the Jews' property, stood at the entrances to the shops or behind their doors. They were openly gloating at our misery. The SS increased the speed of the column by beating our heads and bodies with their weapons, but nevertheless we moved slowly. The children cried, seeking their parents whom they had lost, women clutched their babies close to their bodies and found it extremely difficult to march, many of the sick and elderly fell down exhausted but we were ordered to continue walking; it was forbidden to leave the ranks and help them. An old man fell down and was kicked by a German boot that flung him directly into the ditch, so as not to disrupt the order. He did not get up again.

We continued to walk with difficulty, and little by little rid ourselves of the meager belongings we still had. Every few steps someone dropped a suitcase, a bundle, and another and another one, to make the walking a little less difficult. The street behind us was strewn with bags and suitcases. We were walking extremely slowly; we were confused, stunned, and frightened because of everything that was happening around us, and we were filled with the terrible fear of not knowing what awaited us. The four of us exchanged glances all the way and took care to stay together. We had no words to describe what our eyes had seen, and did not speak one word, not even in a whisper.

A few days earlier rumors had reached us that thousands of Jews residing in surrounding villages and small towns were now concentrated at the brick factory yard. No one knew what was going on there and why they had been concentrated there. From the direction of the march we knew that our turn had come.

When we reached the yard it was already crowded with Jews, men and women of all ages; they had no idea what was happening or what to do. Only their eyes spoke.

We all still had a bit of food left, but the real problem was the lack of water. Thirst tormented us and for the first time in my life I discovered how hard it is to be without water, and that thirst can be worse than hunger.

I thought about the religious people and their prayers, and realized that Judaism was a just religion, because even on Yom Kippur the rabbis would allow those who fasted to drink water if necessary, since it is considered to be saving an endangered life. We felt the terrible misery of thirst on our own skin. It was a hot and stifling day, and there was not a drop of water.

I have forgotten many of the things that happened during that period, among them dates, but it seems to me that all this happened during Passover. I looked up to the heavens; the clouds had dispersed, and the skies were blue. I prayed for rain, so that we would at least have a few drops of water. The worst thing was the unavoidable need to relieve ourselves. The improvised facility was perhaps suitable for people who lived in previous centuries, but now it was intended for us. The privy was open, and visible to all. It was a primitive facility: a deep pit covered by a board, which you could lean on both sides, and thus relieve yourself. Despite the urgent need, which was at times painful and made me feel that my stomach was bursting as my bladder swelled, I continued to hold back. And when I felt I could no longer hold back and began to urinate against my will, we went, a few friends together, and hid one another with our bodies. There, in the improvised privy something unbelievable happened. I was still holding on to the board so as not to fall in, in vain trying harder and harder to urinate and unable to produce even a single drop. Against my will, I looked beneath me, and saw an amazing and surrealistic sight. In this pit filled with feces I could see the gleam of gold rings, precious stones, jewelry of all sorts, covered by numerous bills of money. The brutal searches performed by the Germans convinced the wealthy ladies, who knew that they would no longer wear their jewelry, to hurry and dispose of it. This was their sweet revenge.

Fortunately I had stopped menstruating in the ghetto. Later, the food the Germans gave us contained medication to prevent menstruation. Under these sub-human conditions it was a blessing.

CHAPTER FIVE

Auschwitz-Birkenau

In the meantime, the railway nearby carried wagons, night and day, that were filled with people and we had no idea of their destination. One day, a train stopped at the nearby brick factory and did not move. It was our turn. The moment the train stopped we heard shouts, orders, and curses and we were beaten and whipped as we were hurried into the wagons. More and more people were counted and shoved inside, like animals. When the German soldier reached a number that satisfied him—eighty or ninety men, women, and children—the door was slammed shut.

Conditions were terribly crowded. My mother, sisters, and I clutched each other's hands, keeping contact between the four of us. Due to the crush of bodies, I stood on one leg with the other pressed to it. Many of the people were so tired that they had to sit on the floor and so the crush worsened. Every now and again both men and women rose from their places and moved to the sides of the wagon's door, where the toilet buckets stood. We heard a long blast of the engine's whistle and the train began its journey. Had we at least felt that the train was moving, that something was happening—but it crawled forward very slowly. Then without warning, without us knowing why, it slowed down and came to a halt. We thought that perhaps we'd arrived at a station and I tried vainly to search for a station name in the darkness to see where we were. No station—nothing. The train stood in the darkness amid open fields when the doors were opened and the people standing next to them emptied the buckets, the corpses were thrown out, and the train continued on its way without a guard flagging it off and without a whistle.

I have a memory of that journey that won't leave me. There was a woman standing next to me holding a baby who was crying all the time. She gave the child her breast that had either dried up or her milk was bitter, for the baby pushed the nipple away with its tiny hand and went on crying weakly. The young mother looked at us, apologizing that she was unable to stop her thirsty baby's crying, but the child refused her breast. I was standing next to a small ventilation aperture the wagon had for the animals it used to carry, which was covered with barbed wire to prevent our escape. The baby's cries grew weaker until they sounded like a whispered moan, until it seemed that the heavens had heard its prayer and rain began to fall. What a stroke of luck! I put my cupped hand through the aperture as far as I could and the raindrops rolled down my fingers into the palm of my hand, and I carefully carried the water to the baby's lips. He licked up the water and fell asleep for a few moments in his mother's arms. I saw a look of silent gratitude on her face.

We traveled for at least three or four days and then heard a long whistle from the engine and I felt the train slowing down. I could see a big iron gate and the slogan over it that greeted us: *Arbeit Macht Frei* [Work Makes You Free].

I had reached the hell on earth known as Auschwitz.

I was mindful of one thing: The four of us must stay together. Here, in the middle of the night at the place to which we had been brought, there was great activity as if it were daytime. Huge floodlights illuminated the whole area with a blinding, irritating light. SS officers roared orders, accompanying them with curses and blows. I could see men dressed in striped prison garb, the "old lags" as we were soon to find out, who told us what we had to do.

We were confused and frightened and didn't know what was happening. We moved forward a little further and saw "hills" that sprouted on both sides, to whose height our cases and bundles were added. We were incapable of thought, lifeless figures doing the same things that those who had gone before us had done. We threw what was left in our hands onto the pile and now, empty handed, faced the next stage that would be even more painful. An SS man stood at the head of the line ordering the men to one side and the women to the other.

The four of us were still together but as the line moved slowly forward we were frightened by the prospect of separation. This time they took the younger women to one side and the older ones to the other. We young girls were sent to one side and it was then that I felt that Mother had been torn from my arms. Until that moment we had held on to her with all our might and now I could no longer see her. The speed at which it all happened was unbearable and we were unable to even give Mother a farewell glance. The "Turkish" workers saw us weeping and tried to console us by telling us we would be able to see each other every Sunday. False promises.

The rumors spread like brushfire and only a few minutes later I knew that I would never see Mother again. Everyone sent to the line she had joined was destined for the crematoria, the ovens. The three of us wept bitterly and I was very angry with myself. I was unable to digest the fact that Mother was not with us and I was convinced that it was all my fault for if I had only taken her mourning scarf from her head, which she had begun wearing a year earlier after Father's death, she would have stayed with us. She was a good-looking woman who looked younger than her years and only the scarf had made her look older. I was tormented by guilt. Why hadn't I removed her scarf? Had it not been for the scarf we would still have been holding her hand.

From this point onward everything happened very quickly. I didn't even have a chance to mourn the great loss of my mother. In pain and sorrow I said goodbye to her in my heart as everything went ahead according to plan. The Germans loved order and precision and as if on a conveyor belt we were pushed from station to station, and at each one I was separated from something that was mine. First I was ordered—like everyone else—to take off all my clothes and throw them onto a pile. I felt terrible, I was left with nothing of my own.

I do not know whether it is possible to classify the stages of our humiliation, but at the next station I felt that it had reached its peak. With their rifle butts, the SS men herded us into a big hall that was lit up as though it were daytime and in which young SS boys who had hardly begun to shave but who already carried rifles, moved around. Because of their age, these boys had not been recruited into the army, while we girls and young women stood there facing their blue, contemptuous, ice-cold eyes, as naked as the day we were born. I thought of this terrible humiliation and did not imagine that it would become worse. The conveyor belt did not stop for a moment and then it was my turn. Naked and trembling with cold and shame, I felt the icy razor sweep over my skull and through my hair while I ordered my brain to continue maintaining my sanity. After my head had been shaved, my underarm and pubic hair were removed in a similar manner.

I could speak only a little German but understood everything. I stood there naked, unable to believe what I was hearing. The SS men explained that everything that was being done to us was for our own good because they had to maintain hygiene. Cleanliness above all, they said, and then I fainted momentarily. I knew that with all their dedication to cleanliness they wanted only one thing, to murder my soul. I swore that I would never submit.

Frightened and despairing, I moved around the hall. I didn't know any of the girls around me. I searched for my two sisters and my friends but was unable to identify them. With our nakedness and shaven heads we all looked alike. We could only recognize one another by our faces. We searched among the shaven heads until the three of us—Chaya, Ada'leh and me—found one another. We were still suffering the trauma of having our heads shaved and when I looked at them I was unable to stop my tears: Ada'leh, without her silky golden hair that I loved to brush. We consoled ourselves with the fact that we were still together, and that thought remained with us all the time.

The *transports* arrived at Auschwitz continuously, and the huge influx of prisoners meant that the Nazis didn't have time to tattoo our numbers on our arms, so we were given a numbered disk on a leather thong that we wore around our necks. At the next station, they threw each girl a dress from a pile. I got a sleeveless summer dress, just that. No panties, no bra, and not even a sweater or jacket despite the wintry conditions. Because of my shame and the cold, I pulled the dress on quickly and immediately felt a new, horrible calamity, not because of the dress I had been given or the sleeves it didn't have, but because of what was inside the dress—in abundance. It was full of lice that bit into me and sucked my blood with a million stings; the eggs that had been laid inside the dress multiplied and more and more of them bit into me, so that I didn't know where to scratch first; the Germans forbad us to scratch our bodies. It was terrible, but here too there was no time to feel the pain.

The well-oiled conveyor belt moved inexorably on I couldn't see a thing but the SS men's truncheons pushed us forward, crowding us into a huge hut that they called a "block," a thousand women in one hut. A square concrete block at a height of a few centimeters from the floor ran the whole length of the hut. We thought it contained the central heating unit, although we felt no heat coming from it throughout all those terribly cold days we spent in Block 9 in the *lager*, "Camp C" in English, or "*C Lager*" in German. At the entrance to the block there was a little room from where the woman in charge of the block, the *stubelteste*, could see us through a small aperture without us being able to see her. She was responsible for maintaining order, and for everything that went on inside the block.

I once passed the little room and, reflected in its window, I saw my father's face. I stood there for a moment, stunned. Ever since my childhood I had been told that I looked very much like my father and because of this resemblance, when we were children, my brothers and sisters thought that he liked me more than them. It was not true, of course, it was just normal sibling rivalry. As a mother, I now know that all my children are equally dear to me, but there, as I saw my reflection in the window with my shaven head, thick eyebrows, and my father's features, I could see the resemblance between us.

Inside the block, that held about a thousand women, were two rows of bunks in three tiers. On each bunk, that was about as wide as a double bed, ten or twelve of us huddled together, and it was very hard to lie comfortably on the bare boards without mattresses. Whenever someone needed to turn over, we all had to turn with her.

We reached Auschwitz early on a Friday morning. I remember it well, but later we lost all sense of time. Time had no meaning in that place and each day was worse than the one before it.

All around me I could see the triple-tiered bunks with the girls and women lying on them. I knew many of them—friends, neighbors from our courtyard or from the one next door, and comrades from the *Hashomer Hatzair* movement. I saw the sadness in their eyes, but, above all, I saw the fear.

At that moment something in me commanded me to stir and do something to raise their spirits, and my own too. I slowly climbed down from my bunk together with my sisters and we asked some of our friends and the other young women to join us. We stood near the *stubelteste*'s little room and began to sing. We sang "*Hatikvah*" [Israel's national anthem] with great enthusiasm and followed it with other Hebrew songs, Shabbat songs, and others too. We sang fervently, letting the songs flow from deep inside us. Suddenly the door of the hut opened and an SS man, his eyes filled with anger, came in, flailing left and right with his whip with all his force. We stood there and continued singing until the last one of us collapsed, felled by the blows of the whip. That was my first Friday in the "other world" of Auschwitz.

Just as there are things that happened to me in Auschwitz that I will never forget, there are others I have forgotten, as though they never happened. After everything else I went through, I had forgotten about that Friday, but it seems that fate decided otherwise and wanted this special event, which took place in the block in Auschwitz, in the shadow of the crematoria, to be preserved for posterity. Years later my brother Eliezer heard the story of the *Kabbalat Shabbat* from a woman who returned from the war before me. I didn't know her, we had never spoken, but she remembered me and my two sisters, and looked to us in admiration, amazed at our audacity. When she finished telling her story to my brother, she added that until that moment, until that *Kabbalat Shabbat* in the block in Auschwitz, she had never heard of the Zionist youth movements and that she admired our courage for raising the morale of the women who had lost all hope.

It was dark outside and we didn't know whether it was still night or if they had woken us early, before dawn had broken on Auschwitz. The door of the hut was opened, we were given a tin plate and stood in line for breakfast that consisted of one ladle of an unidentifiable, colorless, lukewarm liquid. And we were thirsty. With the liquid we were given a slice of bread measuring about 10x10x8 centimeters that looked like a cake of soap. This was the daily bread ration. We were very hungry and devoured the bread, which tasted bitter and which crumbled in our hands, to the last crumb. When we were given our next ration the following morning, we were much more careful, each according to her personal resolve. There were some who ate their bread in one go, and others, like us, who ate a little and kept the rest in our bunks until we returned to the hut from roll call. We quickly realized that this wouldn't work because there was always someone who would get back before us and steal our bread. Ada'leh and I ate our bread like everyone else, but Chaya, who suffered from gallstones, was unable to eat it. She lived on the morning and evening drink and the soup we were given at midday, a plate of grayish water in which floated the odd grain of barley.

I saw the electrified barbed wire fence that surrounded the camp. Along the fence stood watchtowers manned by armed SS men, their fingers on the trigger, ready to fire at anyone moving in the area. Without actually planning it, the younger girls like us slept in the top bunks, the older women in the middle ones, and the old ones in the lower bunks. That's how I viewed them then, but there were very few women there aged over forty who had passed the selection and remained with us.

A new *transport* from Terezin arrived at the neighboring camp. Terezin was a "show camp." Those who accused the Nazis of committing atrocities were taken there and shown an orderly labor camp, whose inmates were well looked after—a charade whose aim was to quash rumors of mass genocide. The prisoners of Terezin were eventually taken to Auschwitz with their families, and there they were separated. Like many of us, I stood by the fence watching them, feeling envious that they were still together with their families. Suddenly, a woman standing near me saw her son, who had just arrived. She looked in disbelief, looked again, and shouted, "My son! I'm here! I'm over here!" and as she ran towards him her outstretched arms touched the electrified wire. The guards, who had seen and heard everything, switched on the power even before she touched the fence. Another woman ran to save her and barely managed to touch her before she, too, was killed, and the same thing happened to yet another woman who was unable to stand by without trying to help. And another woman tried her luck until there was a line of electrocuted women lying on the ground, stretching from the fence to where we stood on the parade ground. From that moment every one of us knew that there was a way out of this hell, a simple solution. An end could be put to our terrible suffering in an instant.

The guards would push us into the block where the *stubelteste*—who carried out the orders of the "*Grosse*," the head woman SS officer who was the terror of Auschwitz—hurried us to our three-tiered bunks. In our panicked running to the parade ground for *appel* (roll call), we saw that our allocation of bunks had been correct; it was easier for us younger women to get up and down from the upper levels than the older women. In addition to the armed guard who stood outside the block, the woman in charge also made sure that no one left the hut. I can't remember how we managed to hold on, because we were only allowed out to the latrines twice a day, and even then the latrines were so disgusting that we could hardly bring ourselves to use them.

As already mentioned, there are events from Auschwitz that I can remember very clearly, as though they only happened yesterday, while there are others that I simply can't recall, and this I find truly amazing. Every day of my time there, at least once, I went to the latrine, and I have asked my sister this question over and over again: what did the Auschwitz latrine look like? And she can't remember either. What I can remember is how we were taken each day to the ablutions hut. This building looked just like the hut in which we lived, but with a water pipe running its length and we were ordered to stand facing the taps. We stood and waited for the water. The Germans were obsessed with cleanliness so there was soap there too, a big square cake that I could hardly bear to take in my hand. It was about the size of our daily bread ration and smelt terrible, and a rumor spread that it was made of human fat. It was appalling.

But whoever didn't want to believe the rumors did what I did. I very much wanted to have a wash, so I began soaping my hands. I rubbed and rubbed, but not a single bubble of foam appeared. I waited until the water arrived and in the meantime soaped my arms, face, neck, and body, and then turned on the tap. Nothing happened. There was no sign of water and then three or four rusty drops oozed out, and that was it. Screamed orders hurried us back to the block and we remained smeared with the foul-smelling soap. My whole body itched. Perhaps next time there would be water in the pipe and we would be able to wash off the soap. But when?

After *appel* we were lined up in ranks of five and marched along the dirt road from Auschwitz to Birkenau. We had heard that they were taking us for a real wash and that in future we would have one every week. We reached the ablutions building where we were taken into a strange room, sealed on all sides with a curved ceiling. Once my eyes became used to the dim light I saw that the walls and ceiling were full of holes. I shook from fear and cold. We never knew whether we were to be showered with water or poison gas. We had this "wash" every week, and trembling from cold and fear we thought it would be the last time.

They would wake us up while it was still dark, before dawn. We didn't feel how day was swallowed into night as the camp was floodlit all the time. The woman in charge hurried us to get down from our bunks in the dark and run outside to the parade ground between the huts for *appel*. We stood in ranks of five, always trying to put the older and weak women in the middle. In my rank there stood a woman, then me, then Ada'leh, and another girl at the end. Chaya, who sometimes suffered painful gallbladder attacks, stood behind us. Standing for hours in the same place, in the rain and wind, wearing the only dress we possessed, was very hard and the only help we could offer one another was a few words of encouragement.

Those who were in the front rank had it hardest of all because they had to stand all the time, but the women in the middle or rear ranks could bend down a little, sit on the ground and rest, but this was very dangerous. These short periods of rest were my sister Chaya's salvation as her condition was worsening day by day. Her gallstones weakened her terribly. It was also very hard for little Ada'leh who at only thirteen years of age was the youngest and not nearly as strong as us. It broke my heart to see her like this. She was our little beauty, blonde and good looking, until they took away everything personal from her as they had with the rest of us, and particularly her golden curls, which we loved so much. Chaya and I supported her and always tried to have her stand in the middle of the rank. Our personal distress was very great, although Ada'leh and I managed somehow, suffering our hunger in silence like the rest of the inmates. But because of her illness, Chaya's life was very difficult. She would get over an attack and sigh with relief, only for her body to writhe in pain with the next one. Chaya suffered in silence, without complaining, not saying a word. Sometimes, during a severe attack, she would climb down from the top bunk and sit on the cold floor, leaning against the post that supported the bunks to make breathing easier.

As soon as she climbed down I followed her, to be by her side. One time I woke up and when I found that she wasn't lying beside me, I climbed down quickly and found her leaning against the post, biting her lip until it bled, the blood mingling with the tears that flowed down her cheeks. She bit her lip to stop herself from crying out in pain for she knew that she had to keep quiet, that no one must hear her, because if the woman in charge of the block discovered she was ill, she would be sent to the hospital block. We had to be healthy for the Germans who viewed us as sub-human. Although there was a special block for the sick, there was neither a doctor nor a nurse there and the sick were given no medication and were sent directly to the crematoria.

I knew that I had to find a solution for Chaya who was losing weight daily. One evening I quietly got down from my bunk, made my way to the door of the hut, and saw the armed guard patrolling outside. I waited until he moved away and slipped out of the block. I walked bent over, step by step, waiting for the beam of the searchlight that moved over the entire camp to pass me. I reached the food factory, a huge kitchen with no steps, only a sloping ramp leading into it. The Germans put barrels—*kubelen*, as they called them— out on the ramp with our food in it. I moved slowly, crouching, across the entrance, my whole body trembling, until I found myself inside the kitchen facing the huge vats that were taller than me. They were so clean they shone. I touched one and it was so heavy that I couldn't move it, even though it was empty. I gathered all my strength and tried again and again until I realized that my puny strength was unequal to the task.

Still crouching, shivering with cold and fear, I reached a smaller vat. I gathered my strength again and with both hands I managed to tilt it towards me. My knees were knocking, my whole body shook, and then my heart hammered with joy at what I saw. At the bottom of the vat, among the grits, lay three potatoes. I stuck my head inside in an effort to reach the bottom, grabbed the potatoes and the grits that stuck to them, wrapped them in a piece of cloth I had brought with me, and happily began crawling back towards the door carrying my treasure.

Then, without warning and without an escort of German soldiers, the "*Grosse,*" the terror of the camp, the camp commandant, came cycling up the ramp. She was an impressive blonde woman, her hair gathered at the neck, and her fine figure seemed to have been poured into her uniform. For an instant I thought that such beauty could not possibly harbor Satan, but I knew that it camouflaged a bestial brutality and inhuman evil. I once saw her force an elderly woman to kneel on the gravel as punishment for daring to look her in the eye.

I was still bent over, crawling back towards the door with my treasured potatoes, when I saw her come into the kitchen on her bike. Although I am not religious, I held my breath and silently prayed to God to help me and make the earth open up and swallow me, the vat, and the entire camp. I crouched behind the vat, holding my breath, and waiting for the commandant to finish checking whatever it was she had come to check, and leave on her bike.

As she left I heaved a sigh of relief and crawled towards the door. Again I waited until the guard moved away and the searchlight too. I had no sooner left the kitchen than whiplashes rained down on my head and body—the guard had come back from the other direction and I had missed him. After beating me mercilessly, he angrily prodded me with his rifle butt until I fell, but my happiness was indescribable. Although my whole body was a mass of pain, the potatoes were still in my hand. As I moved towards the block I heard him call after me, "If I see you around the kitchen again, you won't get out of here alive. I'll shoot you on the spot!" I staggered back to the block, my body aching, and just about managed to climb into my bunk. Next morning Chaya saw the red weals that covered my body. What happened to you, Racheli, she asked, and I told her that I had scratched myself on the rough planks as I climbed into the bunk. My sister was so happy when I showed her the potatoes and I was happy that she finally had something she was able to eat. And then, surprisingly, as if it were a divine omen, help came from an unexpected quarter.

Every day a prisoner dressed in striped prison garb passed through our camp carrying a toolbox. He was one of the "old timers" who the Germans employed as a plumber and who passed freely from one camp to another. One day he stopped near us and began talking to us in halting English, but it was clear enough for us to understand. He asked a lot of questions: who we were, where we had come from, and how we were managing to live in this hell on earth. I told him that we were young and still optimistic, that we wanted to live and were holding on, looking after one another. I think he understood what I was saying and we decided to tell him the truth about Chaya—what did we have to lose? I told him that we had a problem, that my sister was unable to eat the bread we were given, she was living on the liquids alone, and that she suffered terrible pain because of her gallstones. Next day he stopped and put down his toolbox as he did every day, ready to talk to us. This time, however, he opened the toolbox and took out a small bag containing a wrapped sandwich of white bread that he offered to my sister.

Our joy is hard to describe, but as far as we were able to express ourselves in English—a language in which none of us were fluent—we tried to thank him and tell him how much we appreciated his wonderful human gesture. We knew that he, too, was living on prison rations. Next day, too, he brought another white bread sandwich for Chaya, and the next day too. We knew from which direction he would appear and we awaited his arrival for hours, happy when he came and thankful for the chance of exchanging a few words with someone, and especially grateful for the sandwiches he brought.

This changed our life for the better and we continued to be optimistic, encouraging one another. This went on for a few days. We exchanged smiles and said goodbye as we looked forward to the following day. One day I looked in the direction of our savior's expected arrival, but he didn't come. We waited and waited but there was no sign of him.

Our initial reaction was one of concern for the safety of the man who had been so good to us. We were afraid that someone might have seen him and betrayed him to the Germans and that he would be punished because of us. I was heartbroken because of Chaya—what would we do now? The days passed in anticipation but our savior did not appear. Then one day I saw him, but he was at the far end of the hut. I wasn't even sure it was him. Next day I saw him again, in the same place. On the third day I decided to surprise him. I waited so that I could follow him without being seen and saw him talking to another young girl, standing close to her, and then giving her a sandwich. I was stunned and didn't know what to do. My conscience troubled me for spying on him, but Chaya was more precious to me than anything else. I was very angry with him and decided that I was not going to give up the white bread sandwiches. I came out of my hiding place, confronted and surprised him.

As soon as he saw me his face lost its color, he stammered something to himself, shifting from one foot to the other and then, in his broken English, he said, "Sorry, sorry, I am very, very sorry." He knew how important the sandwich was to my sister. He fell silent for a few moments and then said, "I know I'm behaving like an unfeeling swine, but you have to understand me. I'm a young man and I've been here for a few years, far from home and my wife, and I'm going crazy for a woman. Then along came this young woman who saw what I'd given you and offered herself in exchange for a sandwich."

My head whirled and I was confused for a moment, but I'd heard him and knew he was speaking the truth. I pulled myself together, looked him straight in the eye, and with a shaking voice asked him, "Why didn't you ask me? You know very well that there's nothing I wouldn't do for my sister." He lowered his eyes in embarrassment and replied, "I know you well enough to be sure that you… that with you… it just wouldn't work…"

I knew that there were all kinds of women among the thousands in the camp and thought to myself that even here, in this distorted world, the fight for survival was harsh and cruel. The will to survive overshadowed every last drop of feeling and at times there was no room for the soul. I kept what he had said a secret and only spoke of it years later, after the war.

Chaya's condition continued to worsen, with her frequent attacks becoming unbearable. I woke up one night to find that she was not by my side in the bunk. I climbed down quickly and found her sitting on the floor. "Don't be angry with me, Racheli, please, but I have no choice. My dear sister, I can't bear it any longer. I've decided to put an end to all my suffering, and it's final. Tonight I'm going to the fence." I hugged her and we wept together, then dried each other's tears and I told her that I understood because I could see her terrible suffering, but that one thing should be clear—if she was going to the fence, then I was going with her. I helped her back into the bunk. Another day of suffering had come and gone.

I wondered how long this could go on. I hoped I could be strong, if only for my younger sisters. One day, on my way back to my bunk, I stopped for a moment and heard the voice of one of the older women. All the inmates around her were listening attentively. Later, I found out that these women took turns boasting of their wealth and the luxury in which they had lived in the past. I stood leaning against a post, listening. The woman was so happy that after listening to nine other women, it was finally her turn to tell her story. She began with a description of the evening dress she would wear at the party to which they would all be invited, her outstretched hands holding out the wine-colored brocade dress, which she then exchanged for a long, black velvet one, which they all thought was fine, and once she had chosen the pearl necklace to go with it, they moved on to the table settings. They unanimously decided on Rosenthal porcelain, but there was some discussion on whether the silverware should be silver or gold, but once that matter had been satisfactorily settled, they reached the climax of the evening—the menu. As they inhaled the exquisite aroma of the roast, the block door suddenly burst open and shouts of "*Heraus! Schnell!*" followed us out to the parade ground and the dream of the party evaporated.

Early one morning we ran out to *appel*. The woman in charge of the block was very touchy and her German superiors shouted orders to hurry to the parade ground for "*selektsia*," selecting who would be shipped off for forced labor and who would be sent to the crematoria. As I ran I prayed that my sisters and I wouldn't be separated and that just as we had left the hut, we would all three return to it. The winter of 1944 was very cold and the Germans already knew that their situation at the front was bad, and their anger was vented upon us. Discipline in the camp became stricter by the day. Chaya had developed a high fever and was taken to the hospital block.

Any scrap of news or rumor spread among the women like wildfire. Now they were saying that all the women in the hospital block were to be sent to the ovens the next day. I wept bitterly and in my heart I took my leave of Chaya. And yet I refused to believe what I had been told. I prayed that it would never happen to my Chaya. I tried to console myself. My sister was in the hospital block and now there was only me and Ada'leh, our family's little jewel. We had always spoiled her and taken care of her and perhaps that was why she wasn't as strong as us, but a fragile little thing. In the long and exhausting *appels* both Chaya and I would support her. Now there was only me to look after her.

The camp was filled with people running about, shouting, a tense expectancy filled the air. The shouting increased in volume, the orders were brutal, and accompanied by cursing and club and rifle butt blows as they herded us, thousands of women and girls, into one hut. In the crush I felt how Ada'leh's hand was torn from mine. I turned towards her, to look for her, and a blow landed on my head. Ada'leh was lost.

That is how they separated us. I was now alone, without my two younger sisters. I wept. What was left for me? After the commotion had died down, about an hour later, we ran to *appel* and when they had finished counting us we did not return to the hut as usual. With blows and shoving we were formed into ranks of five and were led outside the fences of Auschwitz.

CHAPTER SIX

Forced Labor

I was alone and without my sisters, and again plagued by feelings of guilt: how had I let them separate us? We marched on and I could think only about Ada'leh. She troubled me, how would she manage on her own? I walked on without knowing where I was going, nor did I care what happened to me or where they were taking me.

I knew I was alone and that a worse place than Auschwitz did not exist on the face of this earth. We were ordered to move on, and so we did. I saw my new group of five. Instead of my two sisters, for whom I longed, there was Hannah, a young, dark, beautiful girl, who was once my brother Shlomo's best friend, and my cousin Esther.

Blindly I trudged on. The ranks were crowded together and strict order had to be maintained at all times. We were forbidden to step out of line by even as much as an inch. I could only see the pair of wooden clogs marching in front of me, the toes of which were closed, the heels exposed, with no socks. They gave us these clogs on the day they took away our clothing and shoes. I walked along the unpaved road, to my left and right Auschwitz's barracks were left behind; we were moving away from them.

I was miserable that I was left alone; I could barely even think. We continued marching. After a few steps, the marching became difficult as our wooden clogs began to sink into the mud.

I have no idea of the distance we covered on foot, marching in ranks of five. We continued to march until they told us to stop. We were a group of several hundred women and young girls. One of the SS men counted us, and on seeing that the quota was filled, he pushed us at gunpoint like cattle into the waiting trucks. We were packed like sardines, and thus set out on the journey. We had no watches and I have no idea how long we traveled in the trucks, nor what our destination was to be. We passed towns and villages and stopped at a big farmhouse, deserted by its owners who had fled to the hinterland from the Russians, whose artillery could be heard from afar. We entered the farmyard and a halt was called. We stood at *appel* to be counted and were later sent to sleep for the night in the barn, the hayloft, and all the other empty farm buildings. The SS men in charge of us, and their dogs, went to sleep in the farmer's house.

We crowded into the hayloft and lay down on the straw, on which we had stood earlier when we were counted. The straw was wet and muddy from the snow that had melted off our wooden clogs. Each of us was given a blanket that was no thicker than a sheet. We huddled together, touching one another, which created some warmth. One sheet could not warm us up, but several put together, plus the heat of our bodies, helped a little. The winter was bitterly cold. I closed my eyes for a moment and saw my mother standing there before me, so alive. I could feel the moment they had forcibly torn her away from me. And I knew she was no longer living. What would I have done if she had passed the selection and was standing here, next to me? How could I have endured watching her suffer in these sub-human conditions? It was as if I was saying: better that Mother is no longer suffering. What terrible thoughts I was forced to think! I remembered my sisters, and wondered where they were, what they were doing, and couldn't fall asleep.

The next day we were woken at dawn. We stood for the *appel* as we did everyday, in ranks of five, and the numbers didn't tally. Several women were missing. The SS man counted us again, with the same result. We stood there while he counted us again and again—the numbers had to tally. Not even one woman could be missing. The Germans returned to the hayloft, stabbing the hay with their bayonets, searching for the women in the deep straw. Several frightened women came out; they were wounded and cried out in pain, while others were injured and did not come out, and remained buried in the straw.

Every morning a few women were missing. I saw some of them lying in the snow. They were weak and refused to continue marching. I told them they had to get up and continue, otherwise they would be shot. But they could no longer stand on their frozen feet. We parted only with a glance, without uttering a word. Tomorrow the same thing might happen to me too. One day I saw three sisters from the Salzberger family. Our family had been very friendly with theirs. Orders were given to leave, and I saw that they remained lying on the ground, their strength spent. Only their eyes looked at me in sorrow, tears running down their cheeks. I wanted to go over to them, say something to them, but before I took one step, I was whipped and returned to the ranks. (When I returned after the war, Izo Salzberger, the youngest brother who survived, came to me and asked me to tell him everything I knew about his sisters. He heard that I had been with them, and he pressed me for information. How could I tell him the horrendous truth? But he didn't give up and told me he was making preparations to go to Palestine, but had stayed behind to wait for his sisters' return or until he found out what had happened to them. So now everything depended on me. I could not muster the courage to tell him the truth about the state they had been in. I told him that on one of our stops they remained sitting, like so many others who were exhausted, and from then on I had lost touch with them. It was a half-truth.)

Our numbers were dwindling. Every time we were counted we saw the empty places of those who were no longer with us, since we had to fill the groups of five before every march. This is how we knew exactly who remained. We were glad that the cold, wintry days were short, and since there were fewer daylight hours, we had fewer hours of marching.

One day, after marching for several hours, we stopped at another deserted farmyard in an open field, far from any town or village. Its owners, like all the others, had fled from the Russians. An armed German was standing at the gates. At first glance he looked like a monster—his expression was ruthless, his jaw protruded, he was angry that our marching had been slow, causing him to have to wait. He counted us as we entered and sent us to the granary, barn, stables, and any other deserted building, to sleep for the night. The Germans and their dogs went off to the farmer's house. The next morning, after *appel*, without searching for the missing, we went out of the gate. This time we were headed in the opposite direction. We marched for approximately an hour and heard the rumble of distant artillery. At first we thought that we had heard thunder, but as we advanced, the sounds became clearer. We knew that it was Russian artillery.

We reached a deserted place where they stood us along a line marked on the ground. They gave us tools and ordered us to begin digging. We had to be careful to dig to precise measurements. The ditches had to be four meters wide, and four and a half meters deep. As we dug deeper, we had to leave projections in several places, which we used as steps. I was given a heavy pickaxe that I could hardly lift. With my first blow I was covered in a rain of ice splinters mixed with earth, which blinded me and injured my face.

The moment we stopped to catch our breath, one of the trained dogs, fangs bared, would run toward us. The work was grueling. Upon our return from the fields the German guard was awaiting us at the gates. His cruelty went beyond the call of duty. While counting us, he would whip us just for fun. But if one of us dared to look him in the eye, she was severely punished. In his rage, he would deal her several extra brutal blows.

This is what went on every morning when we left for work, and every evening when we returned from a day of hard labor. We would return freezing and exhausted, and as a rule were sent to the hayloft, barn, and any other empty building, except for the house. We laid straw on the ground and slept on it. Until the day I reached this place I did not believe that I would long for Auschwitz, but that is what happened.

I didn't know how to appreciate how happy I had been there.

Everyday we rose from our straw beds, and hurried to reach the *appel* on time. We went off to work in the fields; I wore a summer dress, which was given to me in Auschwitz. The work was hard, and like all the others, I had no strength. One SS man, with the help of trained dogs, managed to control dozens of women. The moment the German moved away from us, we would leave one girl on guard, and the others would quickly climb down into the ditch; we would hug one another, move our feet in order to make the blood circulate, and warm up. At grueling moments such as these, I was convinced that no one in the whole world knew how hard I was working. Nighttime was worst of all. As if hard work during the day was not enough, all through the night I continued working—digging anti-tank ditches in my dreams. Above me stood the SS man, urging me with his gun to work faster and faster, and despite the biting cold I would wake up covered in sweat, exhausted from my nightmares.

After the war, while searching for the place where I had worked, I went to Yad Vashem in Jerusalem where I discovered that I had been no more than a small cog in a vast machine, that I was not alone, and that the group of women I was with was not the only one. Thousands of men and women had worked under arduous conditions, preparing anti-tank ditches, the purpose of which was to trap the tanks of the Russian enemy.

I stayed awake in the hayloft and couldn't shut my eyes. I wanted to rest but was afraid that my nightmares would return to haunt me. Suddenly I heard voices. I didn't know whose they were or where they were coming from. They came closer, and then moved away, again came closer, and again moved away. I was alert and curious to know where the voices were coming from; when they came closer once more, I listened carefully and heard the clear sounds coming from the radio that belonged to the guard who circled the hayloft in which we slept.

I sat up on the straw and made every effort to listen. He came closer to me, and then I heard from his radio the sound of marching German boots, which I so loathed. I listened and was surprised to hear the shouts: "*Sieg Heil, Sieg Heil,*" and "*Deutschland Über Alles.*"

I shook the women who slept to my right and left, and they too said that they had heard what I had, and only then was I sure, since until that moment I thought that it might have been only my imagination.

What we had heard was true, there was hope, a tiny ray of light in the black darkness which engulfed us. We continued listening together and managed to hear the martial music and patriotic marches, which always ended a rousing speech, and which were interrupted from time to time with: "An important announcement for our troops."

"...Our forces are withdrawing according to plan. I repeat: our forces are withdrawing according to plan." At the end we heard the voices again, calling all Germans to hurry and enlist to fight for the Fuehrer and the Third Reich, to their last drop of blood. Again we heard the booming enthusiastic cries: *Sieg Heil! Sieg Heil!* We heard everything and were joyful, embracing and kissing one another. We knew that at last there was hope, a ray of light, if we could only manage to survive until it reached us.

We lay awake as if it were noon and couldn't believe that it was really happening. And suddenly, without a word, as if we had been given an order, we all stood up on our straw beds, stood at attention and passionately sang "Hatikvah."

Our joy was short-lived. The hayloft door was savagely opened, and the bulldog, the beast in man's clothing, wrathfully attacked us with eyes burning with hate. With bestial cruelty he whipped our emaciated bodies. He left the hayloft and we remained lying on the straw, groaning and crying out in pain. I was only slightly hurt in one arm, but at the time I thought my arm was broken because the blow I suffered was intense. Together with other women who, like me, were mildly injured, we comforted those whose injuries were more severe. We helped them dress their wounds with the torn sheets we had collected. We were sore, but excited, and full of hope.

Great Germany, the Reich that set out to conquer the entire world with bloodshed and torture—this glorious Germany was nearing its end. Her inevitable collapse was near; we heard it from her own people, in their own language.

The next day we woke up to shouts and the whip hissing above our heads. We were woken after only a few hours rest, since we had not been able to fall asleep. Again there was an *appel* and again we went off to work. The work was the same as it had been before, but we were no longer the same women who until now, had only been able to muster the smallest shred of hope, with the greatest of difficulty. After what we had heard the night before, the broadcast that heralded the near collapse of the German army and nation, we were filled with hope.

CHAPTER SEVEN

Sabotage

We returned from work in the fields and could see from a distance that something was happening. We were not allowed to go into the hayloft and rest on the straw as we usually did. This time an SS soldier was standing at the door and directed us to one of the farm buildings that were once stables. We were ordered to form ranks of five. We didn't know what had happened but I could see that the Germans were angry and tense and I knew that something was different, something unusual and strange.

We were standing in a long line; my rank of five was still quite a distance from the stables. I looked in the direction of the farm building and could see that the door would open from time to time and the body of a girl or woman would be hurled outside; it looked as if it was flying into the snow, where it would rest a bit, and then the girl would rise with her last remaining strength. Her instincts drove her since she knew that if she wanted to live she had better get up quickly. A short time later another girl was thrown outside and couldn't get up from the deep snow; she remained buried there. The white snow reddened with her blood.

I closed my eyes and saved myself from seeing these horrific sights. But I couldn't block my ears to the heartrending cries and terrible screams that pierced my brain. I felt I could stand it no longer. I had no more strength to listen. I was afraid I was losing my mind. It would be better to face what was awaiting me, to have it behind me—I didn't care anymore whether I lived or died, just as long as I didn't have to hear the sounds that were driving me mad. I left my rank of five, which had not yet reached its turn for flogging and asked one of the girls who was ahead of me to change places. She gave me a curious look, not understanding, and must have thought that I had lost my mind. And, quick as a bullet, she hurried to the back of the line before I changed my mind. She reached my place, glad to be as far as possible from the place of torture.

The door opened and my turn came. I had not yet taken one step forward when I was grabbed by the SS soldiers who roughly pushed me inside. When I entered I managed to get a glimpse of the trough where they used to feed the horses. Now, at both its sides stood two young SS soldiers, guns on their belts, each one holding a leather whip. The first one came over to me and ordered me to push against the trough, lift my dress, and expose my behind. The first blow on my naked body, which was by then only skin and bones, stunned me, and I lost my breath. Before I could breathe again the second blow fell from the other soldier's whip and was no less powerful. Despite the great pleasure they derived from every blow they delivered neither of them was allowed to beat me twice, because each blow was supposed to fall on me with all its force.

The first blow made me lose my senses in a way that is hard for me to explain. It was a sort of paralysis that suddenly overtook me. When the second blow fell I gritted my teeth and bit my lip. I could taste my salty blood but commanded my mind not to utter a sound, not to cry or scream like the others. I continued to count. I felt the salty blood on my lips and in my mouth and continued to count, three, four…eight… and I felt relief, no longer feeling a thing. It was as if the emaciated flesh on my backside had frozen and I continued to count, but I felt that I was outside my body and I counted.. twelve… thirteen, and then I felt myself flying. They threw me out of the door and I was light and flew until I fell far away into the snow.

I lay there for a while and felt myself beginning to breathe and my first thought surprised me—I was alive. My next thought was that I was proud of myself. It might very well be that the animals who had tortured me had tired of me because I hadn't cried, hadn't screamed, and didn't beg them to stop. I had not given them the satisfaction they expected.

These twenty-five lashes were punishment for our sabotage, the damage we had caused to the "property of the Reich."

And what was that "damage"? It was winter and we were suffering badly from the cold and couldn't bear it any longer. We knew that none of us cared any longer what happened to us and decided to make things easier in every possible way. Each of us tore small pieces of material from the corners of the sheets and laid these rags on the most sensitive place, the place where the cold stung most—our nipples and genitals. This warranted the most severe punishment—twenty-five lashes.

Many years later I wondered why I had acted in this way, why I had pushed ahead in the line to be beaten and what an irrational act it had been, since not everybody had been flogged. How can I make sense of it? I knew it had not been me who had willingly volunteered to be flogged, but that some inner sense over which I had no control had commanded me to do what I had done.

Silently we suffered the torture and were consoled by the knowledge that the Nazis's brutal behavior was their way of releasing their seething rage, their sense of desperation. We knew that this was the price we had to pay for our joy at their approaching downfall. Only this gloating helped us recover and carry on. We went on working despite our injuries and pain until the day came when we left the forced labor camp to work for the last time.

We began marching, without knowing where we were going. A few older SS men, in uniform but too old for combat duty, were our guards.

Here too only one German guarded us with the help of a few well-trained dogs. They were in control of hundreds of women and maintained order on the march. We proceeded slowly, marching in our wooden clogs along a side road. We passed orchards and vineyards, lovely country houses and well-kept gardens, and our desire to escape grew from day to day. One of the girls left her rank and was shot on the spot. This happened a number of times when any of the women tried to escape. We continued marching; by now they had stopped counting us but we saw those who stumbled and fell in the snow, unable to get up and walk on. Even if we had dared we were unable to muster the strength to help them. Our numbers dwindled from day to day. We marched with no food at all. Luckily the heavens sent down a few flakes of snow, which I caught in both hands and chewed. It quenched my thirst and slightly eased the hunger pangs that were noisily rumbling in my stomach.

Like white feathers the large snowflakes continued to fall, making "heels" on our wooden clogs, which became higher and higher, hindering our marching. A day or two later a horse-drawn wagon stopped near us. The wagon driver, who looked like an elderly villager, got up from his seat and gave each of us a few small, nut-sized potatoes. They called them *Pel kartoffel* and they were covered in straw and dung from the wagon. We ate the tiny potatoes with great zest, the skins, straw, dung and all, and they were a delicacy for us. We chewed them very slowly to get as much pleasure out of them as possible. The farmer never knew how much we thanked him in our hearts for his good deed.

CHAPTER EIGHT

Escape from the Death March

We walked for eight days without food or water. There were rumors that we were being taken to Berlin as hostages, in case the Allies decided to bomb and demolish the capital. (I learned later that I was one of the thousands who were on the "Death March.")

As bitter as they were, the days nevertheless passed, bringing no change. Many of us stumbled along the way, freezing, some sat down and awaited the end that would bring them relief. Many despaired and, feeling helpless, put an end to their struggle to survive. My cousin Esther, my brother's friend Hannah, and I continued to march, walking at a snail's pace by day, and stopping towards evening at a village or deserted farmhouse, preparing to spend the night there. Everywhere we stopped, the women and girls ran ahead with their last bit of strength, disregarding those who had fallen by the wayside, too weak to go on. They had only one concern—to reach the barn, or granary, or stables first. They would crowd in with the little strength they could still muster, trying to get in as far as they could, to the innermost part of the granary, as far from the entrance as possible. The doors of the barn were not fully closed. There were gaps at the bottom through which the cold and wind and snowflakes would penetrate.

These days of suffering went on and on. We couldn't even think about what was happening to us. Everyday I would repeat the day of the week, lest I forget. I found it extremely hard to think clearly; my stomach did not cease rumbling and the freezing weather continued. I knew exactly the number of days we had marched since I had begun counting them on our first day. It was already the eighth day of this pointless march…

The group of five that marched in front of me was made up of women from my hometown. I knew one of them—her parents had a bakery, and everyday on the way home from school I would pass it, inhaling the aroma of the freshly baked bread I so loved, and still love today. Their daughter's name was Olga, but relatives and close friends called her Oli. She marched at the left of her rank, I marched directly behind her, the farthest left in my own group. She had once been considered the town's beauty. She was blonde and blue eyed, her posture was upright, and when she smiled, which she often did, her smile was cheerful, deepening the dimples in her cheeks. She was a warm person with a sense of humor, easy to befriend, and very popular among the girls and anyone else with whom she came into contact.

I noticed that most of the time the German guard would walk next to her, almost joining her group of five. He was the only guard, advanced in age, and assisted, if necessary, by the trained dogs that were at his disposal. Once I saw him taking out his sandwich, and before biting into it he divided it in two, and gave half to Olli. I found this hard to believe. We knew that their food was also strictly rationed, and here was a man who shared his food with a Jew. He tried to do this secretly, and I couldn't believe it. He continued to bring her a sandwich—it might even have been every day. He was risking his life, but he knew that except for the dogs there was no one around, and he could trust the dogs' loyalty…

Olli and the German marched together as if they knew one another, like friends, and conversed openly, despite the fact that I was walking directly behind them. In the monotony of this aimless march they aroused my curiosity. I wanted to hear what they were saying. The wind hindered my eavesdropping, and only isolated words reached me, but I did manage to discern that she and her willpower impressed him. Their interaction seemed bizarre—a sincere conversation between a Jew and a German on duty? This time I let myself eavesdrop. I pricked up my ears in order to hear every word. When the wind picked up, the words were blurry and indistinct, but when it passed I heard him speaking slowly, in a fatherly tone, and one sentence was clear. He said to her: "…I don't understand you, why are you continuing to walk on with all the rest, do you have any idea where we are taking you? Where you will end up?" My curiosity was aroused, the wind had subsided and only the squeaking sounds of our walking in the frozen snow could be heard.

"…So please, you tell me, what do you think, how much longer can you walk like this, with no food, dressed as you are?"

He was silent for a while and then I heard him again.

"… Why don't you run away?" he said to her. "I promise you that if I am forced to shoot, I will give you enough time to escape, and only later will I aim and fire into the air. Believe me, I won't hurt you." Could this be? Was he telling the truth? While I was still suspiciously weighing his words, I heard him say: "… We are close to the Oder River, it's only a short distance away. The river will be frozen in such cold weather. You can cross it on foot, it will be like taking a walk, and a short while later, you'll reach the other side, and there the Russians are in control. Then you'll be free."

I thought to myself that this couldn't be true. A German saying this to a Jew? I looked at Olli—she was taller than me—and I could see her shaking her head, telling him that she would not go. He asked her why, she hesitated and then said that she was very frightened and would not go anywhere alone.

I heard the German's reply and was convinced that he indeed spoke the truth: "…Believe me, I am telling you the truth, why are you continuing with this march, what will happen to you?" I listened so I would be able to believe him. He continued, "I would willingly and happily join you. I've been fed up with this war for a long time, but I know very well that the moment the Russians see me in my uniform, they'll kill me, with no hesitation, no questions asked." If, until this moment I thought I was dreaming or hallucinating or questioning his sincerity, I now changed my mind. I believed every word he said and told my cousin Esther and friend Hannah, who marched alongside me. I told them all I had heard. From that moment we felt a beam of light signaling to us. We knew that this was the moment to take action. We remembered what the German had said when he saw Olli's hesitation. He had said to her: "What have you got to lose?"—and he was right. We had nothing to lose.

Even the thought that all we had to do to become free was to cross the frozen river seemed like a dream. Suddenly we were flooded with energy and strength, as if we hadn't been starved for the past eight days. My heart was pounding with joy. All at once the three of us were elated, and didn't even feel the strenuous walking or the cold. We had heard rumors of girls who tried to escape, and when passing a farmer's garden, they had crawled under the fence, and almost succeeded. But this attempt, like so many others, failed too. They were all caught by soldiers or villagers who returned them to the column or shot them on sight. We decided that we had to act while we were still alert. We immediately began to plan our escape. The first thing we did was to change our names to names that had an Aryan, and not a Jewish, ring. My cousin Esther, who was the oldest among us, became Olga from that moment on, Hannah became Anna, and my name was Lilli. Whether we needed to or not we deliberately called one another by our new names in order to get used to them and responded to them without hesitation. We thought that we might meet someone who would ask us for identification before we reached the river. We did not know exactly where we were, who would be lying in wait, and what areas we would have to pass through, before reaching the river. While we trained ourselves in using our new names, we began inventing our cover story. We made up personal biographies. Olga began the story, and we would add to it. We joined word to word and sentence to sentence until we agreed that the story was simple, plausible and consistent.

We were three Hungarian fascists, loyal to the Fuehrer. When the Russians reached and occupied our region we left everything behind and fled. We needed this part of the story in order to explain our miserable appearance, as we were still dressed in the only clothes we were given at Auschwitz, wrapping ourselves in a blanket. We covered our shaven heads with a kerchief made from scraps of sheets; we pulled out a few short curls that had begun to grow on our foreheads. We decided to say that on our long journey we could not always find a place to sleep, and one night were forced to sleep in one of the houses along the way. The next morning we discovered that the people in whose house we had stayed had taken everything away from us, all our clothing and money. We were left penniless.

We thought ahead, trying to take every possible scenario into account. What would we do if we met people who would ask us questions? We decided that only "Olga" would do the talking. We would remain silent. We understood every word of German, and could also speak a little. But we preferred that Olga do the talking since she had matriculated in German and had a sound knowledge of the language. We relied on her intelligence, her ability to improvise, and her initiative. We were also afraid to speak because our German was slightly affected by Yiddish. It was important for us to be silent. This was the only way we would avoid falling into the trap of giving conflicting answers, which might arouse suspicions.

From the moment we began our preparations we no longer noticed our cracked lips that stung in the cold or our rumbling stomachs. We had a purpose and, more importantly, hope. We were engrossed in our new "act." While marching we would speak to one another using only our new names. When we stopped for the night, we hadn't noticed that the day had gone by. This time, unlike the previous days, the three of us took care to ascertain where we were. When we turned into the farmyard, we assessed the distance to the road. We saw a big yard enclosed by a double fence, a high barbed-wire outer fence, and a lower wooden-slatted inner fence, and a regular fence separating the houses from the yard. We studied every detail, and etched them in our memory. As always, when stopping for the night, all the women hurried to find a good spot, deep in the barn. We acted according to our plan. This time the three of us were "polite." We kept to one side, waited for all the others to go in, and were the last to enter the hayloft. The German guards set pails near the entrance to the barn, in which we could relieve ourselves during the night. They locked the doors behind us and went to sleep in the farmer's house together with their dogs. I was glad to see that the guard did not lock us in with a key—rather, he used a wooden stick that he passed through the iron rings, one ring in the wall, the other in the door.

When we entered the hayloft the women were worn out and most of them fell exhausted onto the straw. Those who still had some strength crowded towards the back. All night long there was not a moment of silence, coughing was incessant, sleep was light. The women would wake up from their nightmares confused, not knowing where they were. We lay close to the entrance. The women would come to relieve themselves in the overflowing pails near us, and the smell was terrible. I blocked my nose because I couldn't breathe. They looked at us in amazement, not understanding why we had remained close to the entrance, in the bitter cold, in the puddle that grew larger, not looking for a better place like the others. Some of them asked us why we were so stubborn. I heard several women saying, who did we think we were, was it beneath us to act like everyone else? And what would happen if we opened the gate to relieve ourselves, they said in fear, thus causing them more trouble? The Germans with their bloodthirsty dogs would be upon us at once. One older sickly woman crawled near us—she wasn't angry and spoke amiably. She begged us to be understanding and not cause any additional trouble. We had to be extremely strong, listen, not respond, and ignore all this talk. Our eyes grew accustomed to the darkness in the barn. Near us on the floor we discerned the farmer's toolbox. We took out a large hammer and a coil of string—a real treasure. We sat down on the floor and wound the string around our wooden clogs, so as not to lose them on the way.

We knew that time was of the essence and that we had to take advantage of the dark. I remembered our neighbor's daughters, who were among our group, and crawled over to them before leaving. I found the older sister and whispered our plans in her ear. I told her that if they did not hear any shooting it was a sign that our escape had been successful, and we would wait for them on the road. Olga got up from where she was lying, and we immediately heard muffled sounds, voices, and whispers behind her. We had aroused uneasiness among the women who saw us at the entrance. We removed the hammer from the toolbox, and one after the other we banged on the wooden stick with all our might. And then suddenly, in the silence of the night, we heard the squeaky noise of the rusty hinges moving and the door opened wide onto a snowy white night. My heart beat like a hammer. The women were awake, silent in their fear. The door was open and we were standing at the entrance. I thought I could see the German guard and his dogs, but they were only a figment of my imagination. The shot I heard was also my imagination playing tricks. The three of us waited silently at the open door and did not budge. I was the youngest; trembling all over I slowly moved my foot beyond the door. The snow squeaked under my clogs. It was still not too late. I could still withdraw my foot and retreat. All was silent. No Germans, no dogs. Slowly I moved my other wooden clog, sliding it over the squeaking snow beneath me…

Both my feet were outside the barn. Silence. I pressed my back against the wall and walked slowly on, placing one foot in front of the other and imagined during those seconds that seemed like eternity, the dogs' bare fangs, which would soon tear me to pieces. I don't know whether I imagined it or whether I really did hear a shot fired in my direction, a shot that would put an end to my life. I waited, frozen in my tracks, and nothing happened. My back was pressed against the wall, there were no shots, no dogs, and only then did I dare look back, and breathed a sigh of relief. I saw

Olga and Anna, their backs pressed against the hayloft wall. Thus we slowly continued with our backs to the wall, and then the wall came to an end. There was no more shelter. Now we were visible. Fortunately it was dark. A short distance away we could see the low fence, but in order to reach it we had to cross the yard. We had no alternative. I trembled as we crossed the yard and reached the inner fence, which we passed with relative ease. Our next task was to cross the outer fence. We climbed it, which proved a difficult feat since it was made of barbed wire. On the other side we tumbled into the snow, our bodies scratched all over. But who cared? We were happy that the yard was behind us. We walked a short distance and reached the road.

Slowly, step by step, we crossed the road. It was cold and dark. It took us some time until we realized that it was just the three of us now, no more ranks of five. We were free.

We kissed and embraced, joyful as if we had reached a safe haven. We jumped up and down in order to warm up a bit. We looked at one another, still not believing that we were out. We cried in joy at our escape. My eyes also filled with tears of sorrow. I wept for my home and my family. What had happened to them? Who was left? While we were embracing and jumping I remembered my promise to our neighbors, the sisters, to wait for them. We stood there and waited, every moment precious. We had to take advantage of the hours of darkness. We trembled from fear and cold. Every slight noise made us look around: would a German soldier or policeman appear to take us by surprise and arrest us? Time was of the essence and we knew the sisters had a serious problem because one of them had a frozen and swollen leg, and couldn't move, and they probably wouldn't want to leave her behind. There was no point in waiting. We saw a signpost and when we got closer could discern the directions. None of them mentioned the Oder River. We lost the river we had been relying on, the river we had dreamed of crossing, sliding over its ice, in order to reach the Russians, and freedom. We read the signs with the names of different villages and the number of kilometers to each of them. We chose the nearest one. It was important to reach an inhabited place while it was still dark because of our bizarre appearance. The name of the closest village was Thymendorf, which was nine kilometers away. There was also a shortcut, which passed through the forest, shortening the distance to no more than three kilometers. I was as happy as if I had already reached the place, but I immediately felt pangs for my parents and my loved ones. I thought maybe they too had found a way of surviving, as I had, and like me, they too were alive. I hoped against hope. I thought about the numerous women we had left behind; were they still marching towards their death?

Time was critical, and we couldn't allow ourselves any premature celebrations. Real freedom was still far away. We had a long way to go before we reached a safe haven. Only then would we be able to let go. Unanimously we chose the shortcut, the forest seeming the best route as it could serve also as a hiding place. We crossed the road and very soon the trees became denser and denser as we moved deeper into the forest. The constant snow was a source of food and drink, but also a hindrance. It covered the forest trails, and we couldn't find them. We were like scouts groping for the right path. We walked forward when we saw a wide gap between the trees, but after a short distance the gap closed, and there was no path. This was the first time we argued.

Walking in the snow was a slow grind. We were cautious and afraid of every sound we heard. Suddenly I heard a noise close by, followed by a long "cra-a-ack" : a snow-laden tree branch broke off and fell to the ground with a loud noise. We walked quietly in single file, our senses alert, listening to every sound, all the while trying to guess whether or not we were on the right track.

Suddenly we heard voices speaking in German. We waited. What were we to do? We would be arrested shortly, and that would be the end of us. Every faint noise or crow call made my heart leap. Light snow continued to fall and we were freezing.

We stopped for a short rest. Despite the bitter cold I was perspiring from the tiring walk. We got up and continued a bit more, and again I sat down, and we stopped for a break. I looked around and saw a small hill. I thought I would climb it, and perhaps from the top would see a path or paved road. I put one foot down on the hill, and sank into the snow pile up to my chin. All my attempts to free my foot were in vain. At last I succeeded, but my foot was shoeless. My wooden clog remained buried in the snow. I was left with one clog; I wrapped scraps of material around my foot and thus we continued on our way. During this arduous walk in the forest I became exhausted and despondent.

One thing comforted me—I knew for sure that in central Europe there were no primeval forests and that at some point we would reach the end of this one. The snow stuck to our clogs, inhibiting our walking, which became more difficult from minute to minute. We were exhausted, hungry, and weak, and often stopped for a rest. When we saw that one of us could no longer continue we immediately took a break. The snow built up on my one remaining clog, while my other foot was covered in rags; as I walked I looked like a waddling duck. When we rested we removed the snow from our clogs, in order to make walking easier. I would then lie down flat on my back, cooling myself in the snow. I took a handful of snow and put it in my mouth. I ate it slowly, while with my other hand I put some snow on my feverish brow, not knowing whether this was a result of exhaustion or sickness, or both. Olga was angry—why hadn't we taken the path she had pointed to—and as always, Anna would conciliate and pacify us: "Just a little more patience and we'll reach the village."

At our rest stop I lay down on my back, my arms spread out, eyes closed. When I opened my eyes I rubbed them, looking at the black horizon that was turning gray, and it seemed to me that I could see something tall, jutting out against the background of the gray skies. I became frightened. I prayed, please let me remain clear-minded and not lose my sanity. Could it be that I was seeing the tip of a cross? Or perhaps I was hallucinating. I had to keep awake and maintain my sense of reason. I ignored what I saw, kept it to myself, and didn't say a word to my friends.

We stopped, sat down, and removed some of the snow from our clogs, walked on a bit more, and after a short time stopped again to rest. I closed my eyes and breathed in the freezing air. I opened my eyes slowly and couldn't believe what I saw—it *was* a cross, jutting out against the sky and the background of rooftops.

Hope was kindled inside me. I told Olga and Anna to look in that direction and tell me what they saw. They answered almost in unison that there was no doubt, they could see a cross. We were elated. We knew that if there was a cross, there would be a church, and if there was a church there must be a village. Joyously, we danced in the snow, as much as our clogs would allow us, and I was happy that soon the forest would come to an end. Now we shortened our rest breaks as much as possible, full of hope that soon we would reach civilization. At the next rest stop, lying on our backs, we saw day break against the graying horizon, the rooftops, and the cross at the top of the church.

CHAPTER NINE

In a German Village

When we entered the forest after our escape we were happy to find shelter and a place to hide. But now we were relieved that the trees around us were thinning and we were nearing the edge of the forest. Despite our joy we were also worried. The forest had provided us with ample shelter; now we would be visible to anyone we met on the way. There was a scattering of isolated houses that became denser the more we advanced, and after a short walk we reached the village. We walked down the main street and as we found out later, the only street. There were houses on both sides of the road. We looked at these houses, trying to guess who lived there and at which one we could wake up the owners from their peaceful sleep. One house seemed to us to be particularly luxurious and we were certain that the people who lived there would refuse to let us in and would become frightened when they saw us. Next to it there was a small cottage, which looked poor, and we thought that its owners, even if generous and kind, would not be able to help us. Thus we continued and played "eeny meeny miny mo" like children. Time was of the essence—together we chose a house.

We adjusted the kerchiefs on our heads, covered our clothes with blankets, and when we were ready, stood at the door of the house. Olga knocked and my heart was beating rapidly. "*Wer ist dort?*" [Who's there?] we heard a woman's voice from inside. "*Wir flüchtlinge*" [We are refugees] Olga replied without hesitation. We heard the key turn in the lock and the door opened. The light blinded us for a moment. A woman stood at the door, gave us a penetrating stare, and then greeted us with "*Gröss Gott*" [God bless you] and crossed herself. Her hand brushed her forehead, chin, right, and left and then she clasped her hands, her lips praying. She finished and said to us in a restrained voice: "Refugees and more refugees, there is no end to them. And this cursed war goes on and on." She will never know how she warmed our hearts when she mentioned the word "refugees." Without realizing, she let us know that there were refugees in the village and that we were not the only ones. This bolstered our confidence in our story and our shocking appearance. Perhaps people would believe us. Full of pity she told us she was sorry but her house was already full of refugees, relatives, and other people who had fled their homes and she had no room, but promised to find another home for us.

She wrapped a big woolen scarf around her head and told us to follow her. She knocked on the window of the neighbor opposite and shouted: "Maria, Maria, hurry and open the door! There are more refugees!" We sighed in relief for no one yet suspected us. The neighbor also crossed herself and said a prayer and we entered her warm, well-lit house. How can I describe my feelings at that moment, in that warm house? After the darkness we had left behind, the light blinded me, but it was still pleasant. We were inside, we had a roof over our heads. We had not yet become accustomed to the light when the women invited us to sit down at the table. We could feel the warmth from the bricks she laid under our feet, which thawed our frozen toes and spread through our bodies. The kind woman did not cease to show her concern for us. She put a loaf of bread—round and sweet-smelling—on the table with fragrant butter the like of which I had forgotten, and fruit jam, and a big pitcher of steaming coffee. She left the room for a moment and Olga warned us to be careful and eat slowly despite our hunger and the difficulty of holding ourselves back from devouring the enticing food. Later we realized that Olga's advice had been wise, because we heard of many people who gorged themselves to death after enduring prolonged hunger.

We were also careful not to eat too quickly because such behavior might arouse the woman's suspicions. We took advantage of her absence from the room and removed the leather thongs with our Auschwitz number from our necks. We opened the oven door and quickly threw our disks inside; the leather thongs fed the flames and we hurried to close the door before the woman returned. Quietly, as if nothing had happened, Olga poured herself a cup of coffee, warming her hands on the cup, and looked straight into the woman's eyes and began telling her "our story," why we had no clothes or money. The woman listened, all the while holding her head in her hands, shaking it right and left, gazing at us with empathy.

We sat at the table eating and drinking slowly. The woman rose and said that she was going to prepare us a bed for the night. Olga approached her and said that words couldn't describe our gratitude and happiness for her kind deeds. But still, we couldn't sleep in her beds before we had washed and changed our filthy clothes. This was a brilliant move on Olga's part. We saw how much the woman felt relieved. She left the room and returned with clean clothes for us—loose shirts and men's trousers. She covered her head in a warm woolen scarf and took a key ring out of her apron pocket. Briskly, she left the house and told us to follow her. We walked to the end of the yard, went up two steps, and entered a little room with a window near the door that faced the yard, from which one could see the road that passed through the village.

This little room, which had been used by a maid in more prosperous times, was like a palace to us. Our hostess helped us bring in beds and mattresses and we waited for her to wrap herself up and leave the room. Only then did we embrace, laugh, and let ourselves enjoy our happiness. I felt good and something told me that, like me, my loved ones had also managed to find their way to safety, and to survive. We lay down on our beds in the dark and talked about what we had gone through and particularly about the fear of what the next day would bring. It was so good to be in a house once again, and against my will I thought about my own home from which I had been exiled. The next moment I thought that soon the door would burst open and the Germans would forcibly take us out from the warm room, or shoot us on the spot.

I didn't know why my body began to be covered in sores after I resumed eating regular food again, but this affliction came upon me quite suddenly. I called them blisters because they moved all over my body like amoebas. Their color changed from pus yellow to bloody red and they swiftly covered my entire body from head to toe, causing me a great deal of pain and I was unable to walk. I lay in bed and my friends supported me under my arms and walked me to the bathroom. I didn't know what had caused my condition, perhaps because I had stopped menstruating for a long period, or maybe it was my metabolism. I was curious to see what was going on in the village but didn't leave the house. At night I would toss and turn from pain and couldn't sleep a wink. I fell asleep at last out of sheer exhaustion.

"Three Hungarian refugees!"

"Wonderful girls."

"True fascists of the Fuehrer!"

I was awakened from my nap by these shouts. Our hostess had told all the villagers about her guests. My friends immediately dressed in the big shirts and men's trousers the woman had given us instead of our own clothes, which she burned. The clothes were too wide for our skeletal bodies and we held them up with a piece of rope. I stayed in bed, which was near the window, moved the curtain a bit and thought I was dreaming, unable to believe what I saw. The small yard was full of villagers, each one carrying a loaf of bread, sausages, and different kinds of smoked meat and baked goods. One woman brought a bowl full of steaming "*mehl zuppe*," a flour soup that was customarily eaten for breakfast. In no time our little room was full of gifts brought by the villagers, and looked like a grocery store. The villagers had heard the sounds of artillery fire and knew that soon they too would have to pack up and leave. Anticipating retreat, they slaughtered all the livestock, processed everything into meat and sausages to take along the way, and generously gave some to us.

Olga fixed her kerchief, which improved her appearance enormously. She had always had a non-Jewish look. She left the room and accepted the villagers' gifts, which kept on coming. She received them warmly, thanked them all, and smiled gratefully. One by one they left the yard. I saw and heard everything from the window but pretended not to understand a word. Then I saw one of the men who evidently had returned from the front wounded and on crutches. He collected a few men who had not been mobilized, most of them wounded or too old. He told them that the fighting at the front was fierce, unlike anything in the war so far. The thunder of artillery was evidence enough of this. I heard them talking about the difficult situation, saying that at such crucial times they must be particularly alert. Every stranger arriving at the village should be checked carefully. When Olga came in I told her what I had heard and we were afraid. We had been so happy, thinking we were on the road to freedom and now fresh danger loomed. A suspicious hint or one word from a skeptical German farmer would suffice for them to kill us. All day we hardly left the house. We didn't want to see any of the villagers or be seen by them.

In the afternoon a young Russian girl came in. She told us that she was not the only one in the village and that young Russians like her had been working throughout the village since the first days of the war. When the Germans advanced swiftly they reached the innermost parts of Russia where they would concentrate the Russian prisoners of war. Of these they chose healthy young men and women and sent them to Germany to provide a workforce for the farms, to replace the German men who had been mobilized. They called the women "Natasha" and the men "Pavel." The Germans would talk among themselves of their Pavels and Natashas. These Russians came to visit us. They seemed very much like us and we trusted them, so we decided to tell them the truth about ourselves. In the evening when they finished their work they would come in to visit us. We would offer them food and drink; we spoke Ruthenian to them, one of the Russian dialects. They understood us and we could understand them. While talking with them we discovered that we had a lot of songs in common. We would sing together, we in Hebrew and they in their own language. We sang songs that aroused our longings: "*Volga, Volga,*" "*Ochi Chorniya,*" and others. They knew their forces were winning and they were happy: the thunder of the cannons told us all that the front was moving closer and closer.

As our happy little group sat singing Russian songs, the door opened. Our German hostess looked at us from the doorway, petrified. Olga went over to her, put a calming arm around her shoulders, and they left the room. On her return she told us that the woman was very scared because she heard us singing in Russian, but she calmed down after Olga convinced her that we were here on a very secret mission, and told her that it would be best if she mentioned this to no one in the village. Olga once again proved her resourcefulness. We could rely on her. From that evening on, it became a ritual that when we hosted the Russians, the woman would come in, see and hear everything, and leave, but she never asked or said anything. Only the fear on her face said it all.

"*Nashi tankisti yolut*" [Our tanks are coming], the heralding voices could be heard. Someone was banging on our door. It was still dark, in the early hours of the morning. We awoke startled by the commotion. I looked through the window and saw Natasha leaving our yard and running to the neighbor's and there too she broke the news. She went from house to house. Next morning we were lying in bed and our benefactor, who had given us a roof over our heads, came in. Her face was crestfallen, her eyes red from crying, and she said that we should also prepare some bare necessities because the loudspeaker in the village was calling on all inhabitants to be ready to leave at anytime.

She hurried out. We were worried. What would we do now, would we march together with the Germans to Berlin after we had already escaped from there once? On the other hand if we told the woman that we were staying on it would undoubtedly arouse her suspicions, and that would endanger our lives. A few hours went by and she returned. She hemmed and hawed, refusing to look us in the eyes, until she told us that their wagon was overloaded with members of her family and they had taken only their bare necessities; she was sorry but they had no room for us. She expressed her deep sorrow and told us to join a number of young people who were walking because there was no room on the wagons for them either. Without a moment's hesitation Olga told her that we were very grateful and deeply appreciated all she had done for us, that we understood her situation, but to our regret we couldn't walk.

Olga's reply surprised us too. She explained to the woman that I was sick and couldn't walk with them, otherwise we would gladly join them, but they couldn't leave me alone in my condition. I rolled up my sleeve and showed her the sores on my arm and told her that they covered my entire body. She understood that Olga and Anna couldn't leave me alone in such a condition. The woman crossed herself as usual, parted from us in haste, and disappeared into the night. We never saw her again.

In the meantime the number of uniform wearers, whom we hated, grew from day to day. Traffic on the roads was in two directions: inhabitants leaving the village and army battalions streaming in. Their number grew daily. Every yard was turned into a military camp in the center of which was the kitchen tent. Our concern grew because we didn't know what would become of us. I was sick, the village was emptied of its inhabitants, here and there an old man would go by but no one paid him any attention. One day our gate was opened and I heard the sound of marching boots.

We shuddered and our faces became pale. We looked at one another in terrified silence. We knew that soon the door would open and a German would shoot us down. My heart beat wildly and my teeth chattered, when, without knocking, a German officer opened the door. He clicked his heels, looked directly at us, and said *"Heil Hitler."* My heart stopped. We were finished. But the same hand that saluted us only one moment ago pointed to the table filled with delicacies, the villagers' gifts, and the officer spoke with solemnity, as if addressing a large audience: "No longer will you eat food of charity! From now on you are under the protection of the Third Reich. You will work for us and in return we will protect you." He clicked his heels again, again we heard "Heil Hitler," and he left. We didn't understand what was going on. For a long time we looked into each other's eyes and could not believe the "beautiful" things we just heard, but he had said them. We didn't have a chance to consider the absurd situation we were in—working together with the Germans for the Third Reich! It seemed that the rumor that we were "fascists loyal to the Fuehrer" had reached him as well.

The next day, when Olga and Anna were on their way to work in the military kitchen tent, I went to headquarters. They had promised me that among the different types of work there, something would be found for me too, despite my limitations. I reached the door and knocked, but with all the commotion inside no one heard me. I waited a bit more, opened the door, and entered. I stopped in my tracks, facing a huge picture that covered the entire wall. Looking me straight in the eye, larger than life—there was Hitler. I couldn't move, my feet were rooted to the floor. The office I had been sent to was on the other side of the smoke-filled hall. I saw soldiers sitting around tables, drinking and chatting. I waited there and still no one noticed me. I breathed deeply, stood up as straight as I could, and walked across the hall, my heart beating wildly, yet displaying self-confidence, encouraged by every step I managed to take. I heard the calls that accompanied each of my steps: "Look at the *medchen*," "A dark beauty," " A typical true Hungarian." After that I didn't need any more. It was the first time in my life that I was happy to be called a Hungarian. In the past I was proud to be Czech, this time I knew that being Hungarian saved me. Happy with passing my first test I reached the other side of the hall. I knocked on the *feldwebel*'s (the officer's) door, and after hearing "come in," I entered the room. If I had tried to guess I couldn't possibly have imagined what was waiting for me. Before me sat an officer whose sideburns and hair were gray, his face downcast, elbows on the desk holding his chin. And he was crying. I was waiting and he continued to sob softly. He straightened up, dried the corners of his eyes, and shared his great pain with me. He was very concerned about what was happening in Berlin, where the air raid sirens were sounding minute after minute. His only daughter and her baby were there, constantly going down into the shelter. The situation was desperate and no one knew what would happen. He continued to sob.

That was the moment I let myself go. I had held the tears back for too long, never daring to shed them, and now I could cry too, in daylight, and not only into my pillow, alone at night in bed. It was as if a dam had broken, the tears flowed freely down my cheeks and I sobbed out loud. I really had something to weep about.

After work we told one another what had happened to us during the day. I told my friends about the officer. They had also heard from the soldiers how desperate and angry they were and how they cursed the unending war. What really scared us was the growing number of those wearing the hated uniform in our village. The roads were crowded with wagons filled with villagers and their suitcases and baggage. Most of the wagons were confiscated by the military and only a few were lucky. The others could be seen pushing their pushcarts and very many were on foot, dragging their suitcases—the main thing was to escape the advancing Russian conquerors. We were in real danger—what would we do if the Russians, whose tanks were already shaking our windows, were to suddenly retreat and the Germans returned to rule the village? We had no doubts that they would kill us on the spot.

The German officer consoled me, telling me that I wouldn't have much work. "The warehouses are almost empty," he said, "and the much-needed supplies are not getting through. What still needs to be distributed to the soldiers in their posts are a few dozen cans, cigarettes, matches, and maybe something else that I have forgotten." When I left his office I was surprised to see a German soldier waiting for me, a rifle slung on his shoulder; he bowed to me and said: "*Bitte, fraulein* [Please, young lady], allow me to escort you!" I was astounded. I breathed again and was aware of a sixth sense telling me not to refuse him, and I agreed. "Please," I replied almost in a whisper. And again, as always, when something took me by surprise, I was suddenly overwhelmed by memories of my home, my family, and relatives. What would they have done in my place, I wondered, and how would they react if they saw me walking down the street with a German soldier. I hadn't yet sunk into my thoughts and suddenly we arrived back at the house. My loyal escort saluted to me and parted with "*Auf wiedersehen*."

On my return I told my friends about my meeting with the German and they justified my behavior. We had to maintain an appearance of authenticity at every moment. A young girl in this situation could not refuse the advances of a soldier. The next day the soldier waited for me again and this time was more daring. He immediately shifted his rifle to his left shoulder and took my arm with his right hand. I trembled, my skin was goose pimpled, I broke into a sweat despite the cold weather, the blood rushed to my head and my face was flushed. He probably interpreted my reaction as a different kind of excitement, which he liked. I was surprised by his behavior, which was impeccable. He introduced himself as Max, I have forgotten his complicated surname, and he told me that before he was called up he had been a lawyer; his hobby was music, mainly classical. But every free moment he had he liked to read, mainly poetry; there was nothing like a good poem that appealed to one's heart and emotion, he said. He would quote Goethe and Heine by heart.

When we met two days later he looked straight into my eyes and asked me to meet him in the evening, when he was off duty. He told me he would come by and knock three times on the gate. My friends sensed my animated mood, and I told them about my German suitor. They both felt that I had to continue meeting him, otherwise we might arouse suspicion. It went without saying that a soldier was entitled to a little bit of entertainment and my refusal could be dangerous for us all. Evening came. I heard his three soft knocks on the gate and my heart beat rapidly. I banished any thoughts from my mind, got dressed, and left the house. Max was very happy to see me and fortunately he couldn't see my expression in the dark. Two things made my days of forced "love" in the shadow of war easier: the evenings were very cold and we couldn't stay outside for any length of time, and Max had to get back to camp before eight o'clock.

Max couldn't have dreamed of what went on in our little room after eight o'clock. He knew nothing of the young Russians who came to see us. It was warm inside. The Russians would remove their sheepskin jackets, and like onions would peel off their layers of clothing. They were partisans who hid in the nearby forest and came to the village during the day and spent the evenings with us. They asked us who we were and we were afraid to admit that we were Jews, and only told them that we were prisoners who had escaped from jail. We saw suspicion in their eyes and decided to tell them the whole truth—how we had been exiled from our homes, about Auschwitz and the forced labor camps—everything spilled out. They looked at each one of us and exchanged glances. We saw that they still did not believe us. Olga was first, and after her we too removed the kerchiefs from our heads and showed them our short hair that had begun to grow after our heads had been shaved in Auschwitz. They looked at us in shock, and at that moment all the barriers between us fell. They embraced each of us and didn't stop asking for our forgiveness. We did not know Russian but with our Czech and Ruthenian, which was spoken in my hometown, we could understand and speak to them. The village was quiet. The last German inhabitants had left and only the army remained, and their numbers, too, were dwindling from day to day. In the evening, in the silent village, we could hear the artillery moving closer and closer... my friends encouraged me to continue meeting the German soldier. We hoped that with his help we would hear important news. Olga and Anna, who worked in the military kitchen, heard the soldiers talking openly about their situation: how they were fed up with the war, they couldn't see its end, how they cursed the war, and spoke out against Hitler without fear. They too heard the approaching gunfire and we could see their downfall, which they knew was not far off, written all over their faces.

That evening Max told me for the first time about the situation. Until this day I puzzle over what he thought of me and why he gave me his complete trust and wasn't afraid to harshly criticize the German army and regime that were moving from one defeat to the next. When we parted he embraced me for a long time and kissed me and told me not to be surprised if in a few days we wouldn't be able to meet again. He expressed his sorrow that this was happening just now, when everything between us was so good, but there was no other alternative. Tears stung my eyes, it was easy for me to cry. I cried for my loved ones about whom I knew nothing and I cried because I didn't know what the next day would bring. I told Max that I was concerned for him and hoped that we would meet again shortly. He smiled and said that there was an alert, and that the army was preparing to withdraw. The next night there was a full moon and it was extremely cold. Max embraced me, held me against him more than ever before. He kissed me and I continued to tell myself that he was kissing Lilli, my false identity, and not me.

The next evening I heard his three knocks on the fence. I put on my coat and hurried to meet him. When I left I always hoped that it would be our last meeting. Max was heartbroken, he spoke little, embraced me, looked into my eyes, and said that he had to teach me a song which would be a memento from him. He had a fine baritone voice and sang with emotion: "*Ich liebe die sonne, Die mond und die Sterne, am meisten doch liebe Ich dich*" [I love the sun, the moon and the stars, but more than anything—I love you].

It may have been a well-known love song. We sang it together, brimming with emotion and nostalgia. He dreamed of his love for me, but I had my own dreams about my loved ones. One evening Max arrived extremely excited. He looked at me with shining eyes and said that this time he had to cut our meeting short, and it might well be that soon the last soldiers would leave the village. Rumor had it that it would be tonight. If so, he would knock three times on the gate, the sign that he was inviting me to meet him. This time it would mean that the Germans were leaving the village. He kissed me in haste, put a folded note in my hand and ran off, confused and breathing heavily. My friends were surprised to see me return so soon and I told them that it had been our last meeting. I opened the note that Max had put in my hand and gave it to Olga to read out loud: ".. I love you, *meine Lilli*, and I want to live with you all my life, my beloved Lilli. Everything is because of this damned war, take care of yourself, and after the war we will meet at one of the addresses below. I embrace and kiss you. Love, Max." At the bottom of the page he had added two addresses: one in the United States and one in Paris, where we would meet after the war and get married.

Fear paralyzed us. We lay in silence for a long time, not knowing what kind of morning we would wake up to. Our beds shook with the traffic—tanks and other heavy vehicles were coursing along the main road outside the village towards the front. There weren't enough vehicles and numerous soldiers walked on foot.

At night, while we were lying in bed we heard three knocks on the gate. Max said goodbye to me and left the village with the last soldiers. We lay awake, listening to the escaping vehicles, and after the noise and commotion, shouts and orders had moved away from us, suddenly there was complete silence. The next morning we woke up to a new day. The tents, the soldiers, and their echoing boots were gone from the village yards.

The Germans had left and the Russians had not yet arrived. A day passed, and another and we continued to live in uncertainty, in a state of limbo, not knowing what the next minute would bring. It was a cold day in February. The winter sun came out for a while and my friends sat me down in a chair in the doorway, covered me well, and I enjoyed the fresh air. In the silence of the village there was not a chicken clucking or a cow mooing—they had all been slaughtered—and suddenly we heard the noise of an engine. I sat and listened to the noise approaching rapidly from the direction of the road. In the middle of the village a motorcycle stopped, driven by a Russian scout. Like rats out of their holes all the young Russians came out of the houses in which they had worked as servants of the Germans. They covered the scout with kisses and clung to him like a cluster of grapes. The boys and girls hugged him, laughed and cried with joy. He got off his motorcycle and went into the nearest house with all the others. Olga and Anna went along. The scout opened up a map of the area on which the border was marked and explained to them about the army's advance. The boys were immediately mobilized, and the girls, us three among them, were told that in a few hours they would come to take us to the rear. The Russian girls were persistent and finally left with the men, and we remained in the village.

The next day my friends went to the deserted village houses in order to get supplies. They returned and told me a story that reminded me of the morning of our evacuation from home. They entered a house where there were still remains of food on the table—the villagers had left in the middle of their meal. That was the biggest difference between them and us. They left their homes but we were forcibly expelled. The village was quiet, the silence broken only by the ravens' cawing. When my friends returned they told me of a meeting they had with an older German couple, in their forties or fifties. When they saw Olga and Anna they proudly showed them certificates they had kept proving that in the past they were members of the Communist Party. They had smiled to my friends, sure of themselves. Later we looked for them, but in vain. The first Russian whom they met showed no interest in their certificates. In his rage he shot every German he happened to come across.

Armored vehicles and trucks loaded with soldiers, this time Russian, raced down the road and through the village. The traffic was incessant. At times a vehicle carrying soldiers would come to our house. We welcomed them and offered them food and drink, of which we had a great deal. One of them left us a booklet as a memento. It was a "Prayer Book for the Road," with which all the soldiers were equipped. The booklet's cover bore Stalin's picture, and underneath in bold letters the slogan: "For Stalin, for the Homeland." It contained encouraging military marches. We would talk to the soldiers in our flawed mixture of Czech and Russian, and they often burst into laughter when a Czech word reminded them of some dirty word in their language. In any event, they understood us and were happy to take off their ammunition pouches and heavy coats, sit down at a table, and eat and drink their fill. The rumor of the welcoming house on the way to the front was passed by word of mouth among the soldiers. They identified our house by the smoke billowing from our chimney. First they came one by one, then in groups of two or three.

One tall soldier came in quietly, bending his head in order to come through the door. On his shoulders were his officer's insignia and his chest was decorated with quite a few medals. He joined us at the table, eating and drinking, all the while looking at us with a serious expression. Unlike the others he didn't hurry to finish and leave the house. He sat across the table and began asking us who we were and what we were doing in this deserted village. We were preoccupied with the terrible experiences we had gone through and this was the first time we weren't afraid to talk and were eager to relate our story. Olga began and I interjected, and even humble and quiet Anna participated. We couldn't wait to finally pour out our hearts and tell some of our stories. The officer calmed us down and told us not to worry, he wouldn't leave until he heard us all. "Who is the youngest—let her begin," he said. So I began my story, from the most difficult moment when we were expelled from our home; I told him about Auschwitz and the forced labor camps. I spoke slowly to make sure that he understood and I watched the expression on his face changing, the tears that he held back in the corners of his eyes. Suddenly he rose, moved closer to us, embraced the three of us together and said in Yiddish, full of emotion: *"Ihr zend dach Yiddishe meidelach"* [So you are Jewish]. We stood there embracing one another, excited, our tears flowing, until finally we calmed down. He began telling us about himself, his attitude towards the army that was overtly discriminating against him because he was a Jew. We listened, and as *Hashomer Hatzair* members, for whom Stalin had been God himself, we couldn't believe our ears. It was inconceivable, it couldn't be, discrimination under a communist regime? He saw that we doubted him and touched his uniform, showing us his medals and added that he could have been a senior general. He refused to accept promotion, which he deserved, because his fellow officers—when they addressed him directly or spoke about him behind his back—never forgot to add "*Tot yevrej*" [That kike].

It was as if the world I had dreamed of since my youth was demolished in one fell swoop; everything I had wholeheartedly believed in, like a devout person believes in God, suddenly vanished into thin air as if it had never existed at all. I couldn't accept what he said, despite the fact he seemed honest. The officer saw the effect he had on us, the doubts and fears he had aroused, and decided for our own good to put all his cards on the table and hide nothing from us. He told us that by chance, or perhaps it was a miracle, he had managed to save two Jewish sisters from certain death. He had reached them just as a Russian soldier was taking aim at them—cursing and spitting at them, and shouting: "You're Jews, we know the likes of you, you gave to the Germans and you won't give to me?" The moment the soldier saw the officer he put down his rifle and they were saved. Our surprise was apparent. We couldn't believe that a Russian soldier would act in such a way. The officer said that he hadn't meant to frighten us but it was his duty to share the tragedy with us so that we would be extremely cautious in the future. He gave us a piece of advice that we willingly accepted: "…there are extremely good ties between the Russian and Czech armies, friendship and total cooperation. Don't tell anyone that you're Jewish, say that you're Czech until you reach somewhere where you feel safe. As Czech girls you will be welcome anywhere." We later discovered how right he had been.

The soldiers continued to come to our house and we, as usual, invited them to join us for a meal. One day a truck loaded with soldiers arrived at the village. They took over the houses and removed all the valuables they could carry. They came to our house as well. We invited them to join us at the table and offered them food as we had done with all those who had come earlier. They were a jolly group and began joking and my friends joined them. Anna left the room with one of the soldiers and Olga left with another. They invited me too but I refused—I had a good excuse, I was sick. When the soldiers saw that my entire body was covered in sores they hurried to leave because they had been warned about disease. About an hour later my friends returned excited with shining eyes and pink cheeks and told me how they had had a wonderful time with the soldiers. When we were in bed at night and they were convinced that I was sleeping I heard them whispering and I understood exactly the meaning of that "wonderful time."

The next day the soldiers returned and after eating they left the house together with my friends. This time Anna and Olga returned in a terrible mood. They avoided looking at me, their pale faces were downcast, and they didn't say a word to me or speak among themselves. When the door opened the following day they were very frightened and begged the soldiers to leave them alone. But their pleas were to no avail. The soldiers roughly pulled them outside. An hour went by, and this time they did not return. I never saw them again. I had no idea what had become of them. I was alone in the room, lying in bed. It was early evening and it was beginning to get dark, and my friends did not come back. From the moment they disappeared I called each of them by name, time after time, and neither of them came. This time I didn't hold back and began to cry. I trembled from the cold but couldn't get off my bed because of the sores on the soles of my feet. I didn't add any wood to the fire and lay huddled up, cold and afraid. Finally I consoled myself. Perhaps it was better if the stove went out, because if the soldiers saw smoke rising from the chimney they would know that someone was home and they would come in. The road that passed through the village was busy day and night, the tank tracks rattled, heavy vehicles and trucks raced towards the front.

One day a truck loaded with soldiers that was on its way to the front stopped in the village. The soldiers came into the house, shook off the snow, and I pointed to the table and told them in a mixture of Czech and Russian to eat. They ignored the food on the table and continued to stare at me. They came closer and complimented me on my beauty. Daringly, they stroked my hair and patted my cheeks. One of them put his arms around me and I shuddered when he kissed me. He touched me all over and then I pulled up my nightgown sleeve and he retreated in fear on seeing the sores that covered my arms. I told him that my entire body was covered, from the tip of my head to the soles of my feet. He retreated to the door, remembering his orders that warned about contracting diseases, and filled with fear he hastened to leave the house, not even tasting the food.

I was glad that this visit came to an end but suddenly I heard the sound of heavy footsteps approaching, pounding up the stairs. The door opened with a violent kick and the doorway was blocked by a large man, his eyes piercing me. His coverall was filthy and the smell of oil mixed with kerosene and alcohol filled the air in the little room. I saw him coming closer to me with heavy steps and his eyes never left me. He was near my bed and I was terrified. My fingers trembled as I pulled up the sleeve of my nightgown to show him my sores. He seemed not to see or hear and sat down at the edge of my bed. "*Ya balna, ya balna*" [I'm sick, I'm sick], I said to him, trembling all over. Nothing seemed to matter to him. He bent over me, his breath reeking of alcohol, panting on my face, and repeating the sentence, "*Ya khatchu tabya*"[I want you]. Terrified, stammering, I explained to him that I understood his need, I too was a young girl and like him wanted love, but I couldn't because I was sick. He neither saw nor heard, and I could feel his huge hand, like a gorilla's, touching me. My whole body shuddered. He lay on top of me and I stopped breathing because of his weight and for a moment the room was spinning, also because of the strong smell of alcohol. And then with sudden resourcefulness, which to this day I don't know how I summoned, I pushed him off me with both hands and with all my strength. Frightened, I held my breath and little by little moved him away from me, not so much with my meager strength but mainly due to his intoxication. I balanced myself on the floor, the sores on the soles of my feet stung, but I thought about only one thing—I had to run away, and I fled the room.

Barefoot in the snow, wearing only a nightgown I reached the main road. I was saved from that terrible gorilla who lay drunk on my bed. I breathed in the cold air and began to cry. Tears stung my face like bits of ice and my entire body shook. A military command car was racing down the road. When it neared me I waved to the driver angrily. He ordered me to get off the road but I stood petrified and didn't budge. He continued to shout at me, why was I blocking his way when he was in a hurry to get to the front? I stood there, helpless, and prayed that he would run me over and put an end to my misery, and I pointed to the room from which I had escaped.

The driver saw that I was not responding and not moving. He got out of his vehicle, saw me wearing only my nightgown in the bitter cold, took off his long army coat, covered me, and walked in the direction of the house. I saw him throwing the soldier into the yard and with his heavy boots he stamped on his back time after time, cursing him angrily. When he returned he took me in his car and sat me down next to him. Slowly I was revived. I looked at my "savior" and thanked him, "*Spasiba.*" He started the engine and we set off, and I thought about all the upheavals in my life. Not long ago I had reached this village to escape from the Germans, had found a shelter there, and here I was, running away again from the same village, and this time—from the Russians. The driver let me off at a parking lot near army headquarters. I was offered a seat. I saw soldiers and officers sitting at a long table. I opened with the longest "lecture" I had ever given in my life. I spoke Czech and one of the soldiers translated into Russian. I told them how happy I had been when they advanced, how I had prayed for their victory, and I hadn't even cared if I died in their bombing, just as long as they won. And now, it was a Russian soldier who had tortured me. They listened to me and promised that I would still get to know the good soul of the Russians.

I went into the Red Cross station and came out looking like a mummy, covered in bandages, including the soles of my feet. I was loaded onto a wagon because I couldn't walk and they promised to bandage my sores at every Red Cross station on the way. After each bandaging my condition improved and I could walk a bit. I was glad that I was gaining strength from day to day. The war was dragging on, all the motor vehicles were mobilized, and only a few run down cars were available. That was the kind of wagon they gave us and in it I made my way home.

The war was continuing at the front. I didn't know exactly where we were. In any event we were not far from the Oder River, near Silesia. On the way we met other young people who had returned, some having survived the death camps, the partisans, the forced labor camps, prisons, and places of hiding. Some were alone, others in small groups, all on their way home. The little they had they loaded onto the wagon, which I no longer needed. I was happy that I could walk again. We walked during the day and stopped when night fell. We were a group of approximately thirty people. The men went to sleep at night in one of the empty houses and the women in another. Among those walking with me was a Frenchman named Jacques, whom I got to know. I knew several languages but not French. I loved its musical sound and I had dreamed that one day I would learn it. But like other dreams I had nurtured before the war, this one too suddenly vanished. I knew English and a little Latin from the days of the Gymnasium, and somehow Jacques and I communicated with one another. One day Jacques went with one of the young men into the deserted houses to bring some food and warm clothing, and came back overjoyed carrying two dictionaries: French-English and English-French. With their help we could talk a bit, and the time passed more easily. Towards evening when we stopped for the night, Jacques took me by the arm and asked me to accompany him to a small house. He sensed my reaction, looked into my eyes, held me close, and asked me to believe him that nothing would happen between us without my consent. I liked him a lot. He was a tall, dark young man, who was now only skin and bones, but I could see that he had once been handsome. His worldview was similar to mine. He had been imprisoned and sent to the camps because of his communist views— apparently a man after my own heart.

But there was a deep chasm that separated us: I was brought up as a Jew and a Zionist. I knew that I would never be able to bridge the gap between us. Yet my behavior towards him seemingly contradicted my worldview. Equality had always been a guiding principle for me, and rejecting him because he was a Gentile and a declared atheist was unjustifiable. Yet my conscience would not allow me a Gentile lover. Lacking a common language we couldn't speak freely. I don't know what he thought of me when I rejected him. Our friendship continued. I saw Jacques returning from one of the houses where he had been looking for food, with a big mandolin for me, and I was moved to tears. I took the instrument in my hands, pressed its belly against mine, and with my right hand held the plectrum, and with my left the instrument's neck. With the plectrum I strummed on all the strings at once, in a loud tremolo. I wanted to shout and cry and express all the feelings I couldn't, that I was coming back to life, together with the pain that playing this instrument brought to me, against my will—returning to the Friday nights, our holidays at home, when we would sing and play the mandolin and other musical instruments until the early hours of the morning. He saw me laughing and crying but I couldn't explain it to him. I tuned the strings and began playing melodies that were well-known in Europe at the time. I played and everyone joined in singing, each one in his own language: "*Volga, Volga,*" "*Ochi Chorniya*" and other well-known songs of that time. And time passed.

We heard a train whistle and we knew we were approaching a city. I recalled that the town was called Chenstokhova, but when I returned years later to look for the place on the map I saw that I had been mistaken. I have forgotten the name of the city. The trains were working once again. When I heard the whistle I was relieved—there would be an end to my walking. There was a great deal of noise and commotion on the platform, hundreds of people, holding hands with partners, calling the name of a child who had wandered off. I asked the people around me where they were coming from, and whether perhaps they had heard something about my family. Sadly they all said no. I saw the sign that pointed to the train that was leaving for Prague. The sign to Paris was on the opposite platform. Everything happened amidst noise and in haste. The guard of the train bound for Paris signaled its departure and I laid down my mandolin on the platform at my feet and blew farewell kisses to my friend Jacques. I waved to him with both hands until the train disappeared around the bend. I was alone. I hadn't even begun to mourn my parting from Jacques, my special friend with whom I had journeyed, a friend I will never forget, when the whistle sounded again for the train bound for Prague.

I quickly snatched my bag from the floor and hurried to get into the carriage. People crowded the aisles, looking for a good seat and I was overjoyed to find a narrow spot at the end of one of the seats. I was pressed against the carriage wall. My heart was still beating rapidly from my running to the train, but I consoled myself: I had a seat. The locomotive whistled, the train wheels began to move slowly, increasing their speed. I was on my way. I closed my eyes, thinking about what was going to happen, where was I headed, what awaited me when I arrived, and suddenly I saw that I did not have my mandolin. I remembered putting it down near my feet on the platform and that is where it remained when I hurried towards the train. I was inconsolable. I had lost the instrument that was my only memento of Jacques.

As always, I asked everyone I met if they had seen any members of my family. I was pressed between my neighbor and the wall of the carriage, looking at the seat in front of me, and I no longer remember whether I really shouted out loud, or only wanted to—when I saw her.

CHAPTER TEN

Lost Days

No longer caring whether my place would be taken, I rose and approached the woman who had attracted my attention. Without apologizing I said almost rudely: "You, yes it's you, I remember you from Auschwitz, you were with me in Camp C, you had the upper bunk, the third one up just opposite me, I saw you there all the time. You must remember the big selection, at that *appel* when I was selected together with a group of women and sent to forced labor. Perhaps by chance you remember what happened to the women who remained there, in the hospital block?" The woman looked at me and replied with emotion, as if it was happening now, before her eyes, "What do you mean, do I know? Everyone knows, we saw them leading the sick women, naked as the day they were born, we heard their cries, and later we saw the flames..."

I did not hear the end of her sentence. I woke up to find myself lying on a bench, water dripping from a handkerchief that was placed on my forehead, and I slowly came to. In a haze I heard the woman's voice begging my forgiveness, saying that she alone was to blame, that this was her fault because she told me what had happened to the sick women. But how could she, a complete stranger, have known that my sister Chaya was among them?

The devastating news of my sister's death paralyzed my mind. I passed out again and quite some time went by before I regained consciousness. The woman stayed with me throughout, consoling and comforting me. The train arrived in Prague, but I was still in a daze. The woman never left my side, not even for a moment, and took me with her everywhere she went. On one of our walks we crossed the bridge over the Voltava River. I looked through the water to the bottom of the river and in a moment of lucidity searched for something. I remembered Eliezer's last letter, before he left for

Palestine, in which he told us about the desperate situation in Prague, where many intellectuals, the best writers, artists, and people from all walks of life jumped to their deaths in the river so as not to be trampled by the German jackboot.

The woman and I were among the first repatriates, which is what the Czechs called those who returned from the war. The Czechs were true to their character: they were the only nation in Europe that gave me, and all the others who returned penniless from the war, a small booklet which entitled us to a free restaurant meal, a haircut, a night at a hotel, and even carfare for the tram. I learned of these details only later, because at the time I was living in a dream and all the while the woman never left my side. She was with me constantly until we met a *landsman* of mine from Mukachevo, and she asked her to take care of me until we reached my hometown.

In retrospect I refer to those days as "the sixty lost days," sixty days of which I have almost no recollection at all. For the most part, they are lost to me as if I never lived them.

The few memories I do have seem to be a combination of dream and reality. I spent two months in Mukachevo and do not remember who greeted me upon my arrival, where I lived, who supported me, or what I wore. I shudder when I think that someone dressed me, touched my body, and perhaps abused me sexually, taking advantage of my helpless condition.

In one of those dreams I am swaying in a hammock, in a bathtub filled with warm and soft fluff, as if I were inside a huge womb; I felt a man's embrace and heard the voice of a childhood friend speaking to me softly, consoling me, "now everything will be all right, my Rachel, the most important thing is that you are home."

"Clippety-clop, clippety-clop," the horseshoes clicked, and I can still hear a man's deep voice saying: "… and in my sawmill dozens of workers toil night and day, increasing my fortune hour by hour. In my big house, which we will reach in a short while, the cook has been slaving for hours preparing us a feast." I opened my eyes, searching for the voice, and then saw that I was covered in sheepskin, my feet and shoes covered in a warm woolen blanket. My hands were in a muff, which we used to wear during the cold winter months. I turned round and saw no one. The voice belonged to the man sitting next to me on the carriage seat, he was holding the reins;

his whip occasionally hissed above my head and he shouted: "Giddyap, giddyap." And the horses galloped, clippety-clop, clippety-clop on the cobblestone road. At that moment I saw him remove his gloves and with one hand take out a small box with a ring from his vest; he reveled in its beauty—the gold was shining brightly in the winter sun. He continued and said to me: "…Just say yes, and the ring is yours and we'll go straight to the rabbi."

"This can't be, I will only get married in the Land of Israel." The words came from me involuntarily. I said it and was again enveloped in darkness, which swallowed me up together with the man who sat next to me holding the horses' reins. I did not regain consciousness.

One day I took a walk on Rose Street, the street on which we once lived, and with a small stick tapped on the picket fence that surrounded a garden. I was walking along as I had once walked as a child on the way home from school. I stopped and looked back to see where the fence started, but couldn't see. I turned around and there too the slats went on and on, disappearing into the horizon. And suddenly, like dominoes, they all collapsed, and I was walking along a railroad track that led me to infinity. My hallucinations closed in on me.

Everyday young people joined us. They returned from all the different places in which they had spent the war. I discovered later that I was among the first to return, before the war ended, since I had escaped the Death March. Those who returned were counted. I was number thirty-seven. Thirty-seven young people out of a population of 17,000 Jews who had been living in the town before the ghetto was established. Side by side, we would march down the main street and welcome newcomers with joy mingled with tears. My comrades could see the condition I was in and one of them offered to take me to my home; perhaps there I could regain my memory. From all sides my friends supported me and thus we walked the length of the courtyard in which we had once lived. We neared our apartment. The first sight that caught my eye was the stairs that led to the cellar. They were completely covered with crumbling earth. I discovered later that even after the war our non-Jewish neighbors continued digging, hoping to find the treasures that the Jews had supposedly hidden in the cellar. At that moment I could see my mother before my eyes, her blonde curls peeping from the scarf she wore after my father's death. I saw her hiding her meager possessions, removing the earrings I so loved from her ears, putting them into the tube, and saying to us—I could actually hear her voice as if at that very moment she was speaking to me: "So that you, my dear girls, will have something to start off with when you return." I thought of my mother and her message to us to go on, which only her eyes conveyed. I held back the tears that were choking me. I walked from room to room and looked at the gaping holes, where the Gentiles had searched for money and gold.

Nothing was left in the house. We had a small ventilated pantry next to the kitchen in which we kept our dairy products. From the pantry there were stairs that led to the attic where we had hidden Efra from the Hungarian gendarmes. At the foot of the stairs I noticed something white. I picked it up and removed the dust—it was a postcard that my father had sent us from Prague, when he had gone there for a medical examination. At home we saved all these letters in the attic. Now it was a treasure to me, the only memento from my parents' home. To my great sorrow I lost it on my way to Palestine. I received a few letters from my brother Eliezer, who survived the war, and he enclosed letters written by my parents. I keep them in a drawer and often reread them, proud of my parents, and thankful for the education they gave me, which served me well on my journey through life. As I stared at the postcard in my hand, the memories of home that were beginning to return were lost immediately in the haze that engulfed me once again.

One day, together with the other survivors, I walked down the main street, as we did everyday, in order to meet friends who were returning from the war. Only young people, most of them in their twenties, came back—no children and no old people were among the survivors. That day I was beginning to come back to myself and to be aware of what was going on around me. In the middle of the street two young men accosted us and said in elation: "We heard that Chaya too is on her way home."

Everyone except me was happy. I was sure they meant Chaya Marmelstein, my best friend, with her wonderful voice and singing in the ghetto. I remembered my sister Chaya and again closed up within myself and remained silent. My friends saw that I did not believe them. They tried to persuade me that Chaya was indeed alive, and returning home. "Rachel, we mean our Chaya, Chayatchko." My sister was so nicknamed in the youth

movement and at school because she always smiled and was a mischievous
and cheerful person, this in contrast to what they said about me—that I
was serious by nature. They repeated the same words to me, over and over,
until the clouds began to disperse from my mind and their words reached
my ears. I understood what they were saying, but I just shook my head from
side to side, murmuring: "It can't be. I know exactly what happened to my
sister. It can't be."

The moment I returned to the land of the living was the day I was
reunited with my sister Chaya, who had in fact survived the war. I fainted
when the woman on the train told me that all the sick women had been
sent to the crematorium. My sister had been among those women, in the
hospital block in Auschwitz. I found out later that one of the *stubelteste*
came to visit someone in the hospital block and whispered to her that on
the following day all the sick women would be taken to the crematorium.
She had come to save her friend. Chaya, who was a resourceful young
woman, heard this and without delay tore off a piece of sheet, wrapped it
around her head like a scarf and left the block with a utensil in her hand.
One of the guards saw her and shouted at her—didn't she know that no one
goes in or out of this hut? She showed him the utensil and said that she was
only bringing a friend a bit of food. The guard whipped her and shouted at
her that if he saw her again he would shoot her. She hurried off and went
into another hut, and was saved.

Two of my friends awaited Chaya on the platform. They told her about
my condition. I went along with them to welcome her. We walked down
the street that led to the big train station; there was another smaller station
at the other side of town. I don't remember how long Chaya and I stood
there embracing one another, breathing heavily, wiping our noses, and
dabbing at one another's tears. When Chaya dried my tears I looked straight
into her eyes and saw them smiling at me; she was all smiles, just as I had
remembered her, and then I knew that I had found my sister. We proceeded
to the town center and approached the building that was once the Hebrew
Gymnasium. Chaya was concerned about me; she didn't want me to look
at the building for fear that I would become upset, and drew my attention
away. She showed me her wristwatch and told me that when the Americans
liberated her camp one of them gave her the watch as a gift. She had sworn
that she would give it to the sister she would meet first. My sister's scheme

was successful and we passed the building in which I had spent such a wonderful period of my life, while my eyes were glued to the small gold watch with the braided red band. While Chaya was putting her watch on my wrist, she didn't stop talking, not allowing my mind to dwell on anything else. She continued, "You have already forgotten, my Racheli, that we have a brother in Palestine, that Eliezer is married to Pnina, and that they have a son named Ya'ir [He will light the way]." It sounded to us like a new name, the like of which we had never heard before, and to us it was somehow symbolic. We told one another that he would light our way. "And don't you remember, Rachel, how at home we used to dream of the day we would be able to go to the Land of Israel and build a kibbutz?" Slowly I began to understand and take an interest in what she was saying.

I discovered that in Budapest people were organizing for *aliyah* and one day we left our hometown and traveled there, hoping to continue on to Palestine. But plans were one thing and actions another. A believing Jew says, "Man proposes but God disposes." In Budapest the youth movements were very active. Preparations were made to press forward for *aliyah* in every possible way. I was full of hope that soon my dream would come true.

I wanted to hear one thing from my sister—how was it possible that she was here, next to me, when everyone had said that she was gone and that I would never see her again. Returning to her miraculous escape from the hospital block, when she told the guard that she was just visiting a friend, what really convinced him was her appearance. She had a round face, and her pink cheeks, smoldering with fever, camouflaged her condition, and she was saved. I asked Chaya how she had coped with the gallstones she suffered from so badly in Auschwitz. She told me about her good fortune. All the women who inhabited the new block she joined after her escape from the hospital block were relatively young and healthy looking. The next day, during *appel* and selection, the Germans selected a group of women in which she was included and took them by truck to a nearby city to work in an ammunition factory. The factory was of vital importance to the army and therefore the prisoners enjoyed relatively decent conditions. They lived in a two-story building and despite the fact that it wasn't heated, they did not suffer from the cold and had a roof over their heads. Their food was also adequate so as to provide them with the strength they needed to continue their work. Chaya befriended a nurse who worked there, who helped her obtain proper food and painkillers. Chaya worked at cleaning used shell cases of gunpowder residue so that they could be reused. My dear sister, who wrote poetry even in those days (today, her children's rhymes are published in children's newspapers and are heard occasionally over the radio), wrote poignant poems about the forced labor she endured, and how she was forced to prepare ammunition for the Germans with her own hands for use against her family and all of humankind.

After our arrival in Budapest, the first thing I did was to admit Chaya into the biggest and best Jewish hospital. They couldn't take care of her immediately because she had a bad cold. We waited for several days and when Chaya's temperature dropped she was immediately taken to the operating theater. I remember the little bowl on the table next to her bed in which there were a few gray stones. I had always thought that the word "gallstones" was a colloquialism, but there they were, real stones, small and large ones, lying in a kind of bag. This was the gall bladder that had caused Chaya such horrendous pain and made her life a misery, while she stoically bore it all in silence from the days of the ghetto, when the pain first began. But who could have taken care of her then, in those bleak days?

When I left Chaya after visiting her at the hospital, I was approached by one of my *landsmen*. After an emotional encounter, during which we asked one another which family members we had found, I was surprised to hear that he had met my brother Shlomo in Prague, where he had seen him standing in front of a military hospital, leaning on a pair of crutches, looking unwell. But the *landsman* wouldn't tell me anymore and before we parted he insisted that I visit Shlomo as soon as possible. When I returned to the hospital I found Chaya in good spirits. She was recuperating well after the surgery. I gave her the joyous news that Shlomo had returned from the war. My sister convinced me that she was feeling better, was well taken care of, and that I had better leave at once and find Shlomo, whom we had not heard from since the day he was forcibly taken from our home by the Hungarian gendarmes. We embraced and parted in sorrow. It hurt me to leave her alone in a strange city, but Chaya urged me to leave at once.

With only a small bag that held my toiletries and basic necessities, I weaved my way through the throngs of people on the platform and boarded the train bound for Prague. I heard the wheels clanking in my ears: "Shlomo's alive, Shlomo's alive," and I felt my heart split into two. On the one hand I was concerned for my sister whom I had left behind, and on the other I was happy that I was finally going to see my brother. Thinking only of the purpose of my trip and my anticipated reunion with my brother, I paid no attention to the crowds in the carriage and found myself a seat. Later a woman entered the carriage who was almost unable to stand and I gave up my seat for her. I was deep in thought and didn't pay attention to the stops until I suddenly heard a long shrill whistle, and the locomotive slowed down and stopped at Bratislava, the capital of Slovakia. The doors opened, just a few people got off the train, but many got on, crowding inside. I stood between the rows of seats and saw a group of Russian soldiers on the platform, forcibly making their way into my carriage, which was already packed. They sat on the steps and in the aisles, taking up every free square inch of space, rudely and loudly laughing and talking among themselves. In Prague I had heard that they were great watch-lovers. I checked to see that my watch was still in place and hid it from them inside my bra strap. The watch had been a precious gift from Chaya.

The Russians looked around and coarsely approached anyone wearing a watch, extending their hands and saying: *"Dvai chesi!"* [give me your watch]. The soldiers' arms were filled with watches, and they gazed at them admiringly. I stood quietly, full of fear. Next to me, a farmer was seated on the carriage floor, wearing a sheepskin, with a basket of clucking chickens beside him. I stood next to him, pretending he was my grandfather, and was certain that he would protect me if I needed him, as he would his own granddaughter. Suddenly, I gasped in horror. I felt the body of one of the soldiers pushing against my back, his mouth breathing heavily down my neck. Shivers went down my spine when I felt his erection pushing against me. Terrified, I pushed my way with my elbows, desperately stepping over those sitting on the floor, as if I was fleeing a fire. I did not stop until I reached the carriage door and went outside to stand on the iron platform that connected the carriages. I breathed like a chimney, my teeth chattered in fear. In the cold wind that became more intense as the carriage sped ahead, each breath I took was difficult, but my heart was victorious for I had managed to escape the soldiers. "One more victory of this kind, and I'm lost." I was left empty-handed, the little I had in my bag and most importantly, my coat, had been left in the carriage and I knew that I could not return there.

I spent the rest of the journey on the iron platform with its clinking chains until I heard a long whistle from the engine. The pistons slowed their rhythmic motion and the train reached its destination and came to a halt. I was in Prague, the city in which no friend or relative awaited me, empty-handed and with no money in my pocket. I knew the purpose of my journey and set out on foot. I reached a building that had a big Red Cross sign on it and knowing it was a hospital, I entered. A nurse welcomed me politely, listened to my request, looked through a list, but did not find the name of my brother, Shlomo Friedman, Alexander, in Czech. My disappointment didn't prevent me from continuing to look for him. In post-war Prague almost every school was turned into a military hospital, the Red Cross flag flying outside. I went from one hospital to the next, from one disappointment to the next. I was tired and depressed. How would I find my brother? In one of the makeshift hospitals I went over to the clerk, and breathed a sigh of relief. I was finally given the answer I was waiting for. My brother was there and I could see him shortly. One of the nurses accompanied me to a small room at the end of a corridor and left me there. My heart was beating wildly as I knocked on the door. I stood at the entrance. Inside the room a soldier leaning on crutches rose from his seat—an emaciated old-young man, his uniform hanging from his frame, and only his frizzy hair, familiar smile, and green eyes that looked straight into mine convinced me that it was my brother Shlomo. We embraced and tearfully kissed. I had not yet managed to recover from the shock of his appearance, which filled me with concern, when I suffered yet another shock. He spoke to me in Czech: "How good it is to see you, Ruzsenka," that was my name in Czech. "My dear sister. I've heard, I know what you suffered during the war and I am very happy that you survived and we are together again."

He spoke in Czech—a foreign language—and not in Hebrew, which was our mother tongue and the language we spoke at home. From this point on our dialogue was like that of two deaf people. As a matter of course I spoke Hebrew and he insisted on speaking to me only in Czech. He still adhered to his left-wing beliefs, even more zealously than in the past. He spoke of his ideology that strove to achieve equality among nations and races. He was a fervent communist, no doubt the result of brainwashing.

I found it hard to believe what he was saying, and in the passion of our meeting almost forgot to tell him about Chaya. He was overjoyed to hear that she too had survived and returned from the war. Then I had an idea. I hoped to divert my brother from his path and so I asked him to come back with me to Budapest to see Chaya. I hoped that the reunion of the three of us would arouse memories in him, make him give up his plans and join us.

Shlomo smiled at me and shook his head. "Just to see her," I insisted. I told him that a visit from him would hasten her recovery. His adamant "no" hurt me very much. He said that if Chaya wanted to see him, she should come to him. Later he said to me, as if he had guessed my intentions, and as if speaking before an audience: "Look Rachel, now that the war has come to an end and fascism is defeated and no longer exists, why should I go to Palestine? Try, dear sister, to convince me. Why should I concern myself with the Jews, or the Czechs, the Russians, or any other people? I believe that all people are equal. You too were always a socialist, like our father, so now is the time to fight for all humanity." A soft knock on the door and a young dark woman entered the room, wearing a white Red Cross apron, a kerchief covering her hair. She was carrying a tray. "Come here, Anushka, and let me introduce my two beloved women to each other, meet my sister Rachel, about whom you have heard so much, and you Rachel, meet my little Anna whom I love dearly."

The girl placed the tray on the table. For a moment her gentle hand held mine. She exchanged looks with my brother and with a friendly bob of her head left the room, closing the door behind her. Shlomo seemed relaxed. In the past he was always a favorite among teenage girls and it seemed that here too, despite his appearance and poor health, he was no celibate. Despite my sorrow and the pain I felt about his health and the alienation between us, I was comforted that there was someone who loved him and devotedly cared for him. We parted and I promised to return the next day. At night in my hotel room I tossed and turned and was unable to sleep a wink. My heart was heavy. Why had I failed? What had I done wrong? Perhaps tomorrow I would be able to convince him to come back to Budapest with me to see Chaya. Unfortunately he still refused, and I had to return to Chaya, so I promised to come back soon for a visit.

Left with no alternative I traveled back and forth between Shlomo in Prague and Chaya in Budapest. Exactly two weeks after I left Shlomo, I returned to the hospital. I went straight to the little room at the end of the corridor, knocked on the door, and not hearing a sound, entered. Anna was huddled up in the chair and didn't hear the door open. Slowly she raised her head and I saw a look of tremendous sadness and disappointment on her face. She spoke faintly and slowly: "… I was working at the hospital that night; he came to me sick, with a high fever. I took care of him like I take care of all my patients—with all my heart and total devotion. He came to me and loved me as no one before ever loved me, and I had no lack of suitors in the past. He vanquished me with all his love, I didn't know what was happening to me, and then he suddenly left me without saying goodbye. He loved me so much. We made love, please pardon me, everything was so good. When I met him I left my boyfriend, I gave him and everything else up, because my only dream was to live with my beloved Alexander. You can see my meager room, I don't have much, but we said that we would make do with what we had. I dreamed of a little house with a flower garden and we said that even if we didn't have anything else we would always have our love, our…" She burst into tears, couldn't finish her sentence, and left the room. She returned and handed me a rolled-up piece of paper. "After all my dreams and his promises, look for yourself what is left of him. I found it this morning, rolled up in a cup from which he was drinking." I rolled out the piece of paper and read aloud: "Anushka, my beloved. When you read this I will be far away." My voice quivered and I continued to read silently: "I want you to know that I had many girlfriends in my youth… loved ones…like you, they were close to my heart…you know that I have a dream… love…and I must continue and act…I have no other love…when you long for me remember those moments…until my dying breath… with me, in my heart, I love you and kiss you, Alexander."

I read it with difficulty, the tears blurring the words. Anna and I embraced. Even now it is hard for me to describe my feelings, how after all my searching for him, I had finally found my brother only to lose him again.

I sat with Anna and learned from her what had happened to Shlomo after he was taken by the Hungarian gendarmes. First he worked as a woodcutter. He told her how he had run away, crossed the border into Russia, certain that he would be received there with open arms as a fellow communist, but when he arrived he was tortured and sentenced to hard labor. The Russians transported logs down a river. With other suspects like himself he worked in the freezing river up to his shoulders. My brother's friends, who suffered together with him, saw that he was still completely devotéd to the party, which caused him so much personal suffering. He was emaciated and weak and his fellow workers couldn't understand why he continued to passionately preach his belief in the regime. He was sent to Prague to recuperate and even there he did not rest, and despite the fact that the doctors forbade him to go out he made passionate speeches to the crowds.

For many years, whenever my sister Chaya and my brother Eliezer and I would meet, I told them of my reunion with Shlomo, related our brief conversations, and his sudden disappearance. I felt guilty and my conscience plagued me. I was the only one of our family to see him after the war and perhaps I hadn't done enough to convince him to come with us to Palestine. I thought that perhaps he avoided meeting me again in Prague because of his opinions, but Eliezer didn't believe it. The two brothers had a strong bond between them and Eliezer was convinced that if Shlomo were alive, even if he had reached Russia or the faraway Siberian gulags, he would have sent us a sign. My brother Eliezer searched for me and for Chaya until the moment we reached Palestine. Now he continued to search for a trace of Shlomo. He kept that last postcard that Shlomo had sent him from Prague, dated June 28, 1945.

Eliezer was in contact with a lovely woman from Prague. He would send her medicines that she needed and couldn't buy in Czechoslovakia, and those that we couldn't buy in Israel, he would order for her from Switzerland or the United States, and she was eternally grateful. A few years later they reestablished contact. This time Eliezer told her about Shlomo and how he had disappeared in Prague leaving no trace. The woman's husband was a retired Czech general and at his wife's request, went down into the basement, searched through the military archives, and found an important document, which stated that Shlomo had requested a transfer from the Czech to the Russian army, and left Prague on June 28, 1945 on his way to Russia. In the postcard that he sent to Eliezer, Shlomo added that on the way he would stop off in Mukachevo to see if anyone from his family had returned from the war. A few years ago, during our visit to Slovakia, Eliezer received a letter from the woman in Prague with an address of a cemetery in Kromjeziz in Czechoslovakia, where my brother Shlomo was buried. We later discovered that the train that he was on had left but had never reached its destination. We reached the hotel where we were to be staying, and immediately phoned the cemetery office and arranged a meeting with the woman in charge. We asked her not to lock the gates even if we were a few minutes late. We told her that we were strangers and did not know the way.

Before leaving the hotel we rented a taxi and packed it with tools and cleaning materials because we didn't know in what condition we would find the cemetery, and Shlomo's grave. We stopped at a stall and bought flowers, flowerpots, and candles, and set off on our way. We had been driving for less than an hour when from both sides of the road, Slovakian border policemen appeared. They asked us for our visas, which we did not have. When we left Israel we did not know that there was a border between the two countries and we couldn't wait for over a week at our hotel, or go to Bratislava in order to get the visas, so we set off without them. We were racing against time. I began talking to the younger of the two, who was Czech, and half listened to the argument going on between the older policeman and my husband Ze'ev. We knew that every minute was precious. Ze'ev had no patience, took out our two passports, and gave them to the policeman who was surprised that we were willing to leave them with him. He said that the border would close at seven o'clock, and if we were late we would not be able to return till the morning.

We continued on a short distance and only then did we realize how foolhardy we had been. Every few meters there were policemen who asked us for identification—we were lost and could already see ourselves spending our vacation in jail. We hurried our driver, who was tense because he knew that he was forbidden to drive us without a visa, but our dollars convinced him and he was willing to take the risk. We drove speedily on and reached the cemetery in time. The woman who we had spoken to was waiting for us at the gate and we followed her to her small office. We were surprised to find in such a place, among the graves, a beautiful young woman. She was in charge of the cemetery and showed us around. We walked along a row of tall chestnut trees and saw to our right and left endless rows of crosses. After turning a corner we walked a bit more and reached the military section. We saw that all the equipment we had brought with us was superfluous as the place was clean and well taken care of, no less so than military cemeteries in Israel.

I stood by the grave and looked with emotion at the headstone: "Alexander (his Czech name) Friedman, born 1920, died in June 1945." We covered the grave with flowers, particularly the cross at its head, which troubled me a great deal. Ze'ev dug the flowerpots into the ground on both sides. The woman in charge saw how moved we were and promised that when winter came she would keep the flowerpots in her office and take them out again in the spring, and if necessary she would see that they were replaced. We lit memorial candles and stood there, taking many photographs. After so many years, even this was a great thing—I had the privilege at least to weep at my brother's grave. I took many pictures from all angles and couldn't stop. We knew that we would never see my brother's grave again and it was hard for us to leave. In my heart I said goodbye to Shlomo and began to walk away. I turned around to get a last glimpse and saw a small, bent woman arranging the flowers we had brought around my brother's grave. She reminded me of Hannaleh whom my brother had loved in his youth. Then suddenly I remembered Anna, the nurse in Prague, who was my brother's greatest and last love. When we returned to the office we sat with the young woman in charge who told us that we were fortunate. The train on which my brother Shlomo was traveling had collided with an oncoming train and the bodies of hundreds of soldiers were mutilated beyond recognition and later buried in a common grave, which we had seen. Shlomo was among the few who were identifiable. We thanked her profusely.

To return to the post-war days, I traveled back to Budapest to Chaya. Feeling depressed, I told her of my joyous reunion with Shlomo and our bitter parting, or rather non-parting, and the letter he had left for his beloved. We immediately began preparations for *aliyah* to Palestine. We had a clear-cut plan, but the movement leadership thought otherwise. Once again, it was a case of "Man proposes but God disposes." The movement was faced with a great deal of work—the *aliyah* of thousands who were waiting, and we, the members, had the task of remaining behind and continuing the work, until our turn arrived. Thus Chaya and I parted again, this time willingly and with a sense of purpose, that we were fulfilling a mission. Chaya was sent to Mishkoltz, a provincial town in Hungary, where there was a Jewish community, many of whose members were assimilated Jews who knew no Hebrew or anything about Zionism or the Land of Israel.

I was sent with older movement members to an orphanage in Bakaschechva, a town south of Budapest. Some of the children had one parent who wasn't able to care for them. We gathered the children from different hiding places where they had spent the war—monasteries, churches, and other institutions in the capital, and we served as both parents and teachers and addressed all their problems, which were numerous. I was put in charge of a group of ten girls who chose "Homeland" as the name of their group. They were about twelve years old and I taught them Hebrew. They found the language extremely difficult. I sang them songs to accustom them to the sound of Hebrew. In the morning I would play the mandolin, which also served as their reveille. I went from bed to bed until I saw their sleepy eyes smiling at me.

We waited together with the children until our turn for *aliyah* came. Preparations were clandestine and since the sudden disappearance of the children from school would arouse suspicion, they stayed at home and we taught them whatever we could, without any books or writing materials. After class the children were responsible for the maintenance of their home. The older ones, the twelve-year-olds, would bring food everyday from the Wizo women's soup kitchen and the younger ones helped us with the cleaning.

The youngest child, who was six, was our favorite. He was small and endearing and we nicknamed him Big Bill. Today he lives in Jerusalem with his wife and children. Big Bill had a brother named Joseph Chilleg with whom I maintained contact over the years and since he has a brother-in-law here in Kibbutz Yakum, he visits us frequently. And last but not least, Benjamin Hahn, a kibbutz member and neighbor who often reminds me of things that he remembers better than I do.

We were waiting, on tenterhooks, ready to leave. One evening a tarpaulin-covered truck arrived. We uncovered the tailgate and quietly helped the children inside and only then got in ourselves, closing the tailgate behind us. We sat quietly. Our destination was Vienna. On the way we stole across the borders, telling the children that they could not talk at all so that we wouldn't be discovered. One little girl whispered: "How good it is,"… and another child answered: "and how pleasant," and another one said: "On the mountains," all excerpts from Hebrew songs. I listened to them and was proud of their resourcefulness. They didn't understand a word and thought that no one would understand them even if they did hear their singing. The group consisted of forty-two children, myself, and two other women and one man, Arieh, who was in charge of the group, and of our money. We reached Vienna, and had not yet reorganized ourselves when Arieh went off into the city taking all our money with him. He returned a few hours later and we didn't recognize him; he was dressed in the *lederhosen* typical of the hunting-loving Tyrolean, and an elegant leather jacket. He took his backpack and left without a word. He disappeared with our money, never to be seen again.

Our warm welcome in Vienna made me forget that we were penniless. Vienna was a wonderful experience for me and particularly for the children—an amazing Garden of Eden. In retrospect I learned that we were the first group of child survivors to come to Vienna and we were received warmly and kindly by the Jewish Agency, the Joint Palestine Appeal, and other philanthropic organizations that went out of their way to be hospitable.

We were housed in a large house near the Schoenbrun Palace, and in addition to the excellent food and sweets, which were plentiful, they also took care to provide us with entertainment. I took the children to the pool and the famous Prater amusement park. I also enjoyed myself, my cheeks were rosy, and my figure returned to its pre-war proportions. All good things come to an end as did this Garden of Eden, and the day finally arrived when we had to say goodbye and leave for Palestine.

Before leaving we took advantage of the fact that it was a Friday and organized a *Kabbalat Shabbat* for all our benefactors, like the ones we used to have in our youth movement back home. After the speeches ended the children performed, read a stanza from a poem by Bialik, and a small choir sang a few songs. The children did not understand a word said on stage, nor did many of the guests in the audience since they did not know Hebrew. When the performance ended I rushed backstage, but quite a few people came over to shake my hand and thank me for the moving evening, wishing me well for the rest of our journey. We left Vienna the next day.

We drove north to Germany and reached a placed named Strüt An Ansbach, a village near Ansbach. There was an organized school there, the teachers, mainly volunteers from Palestine, who worked with great dedication to their task. After school hours, the children were divided into groups according to the various youth movements. I was a counselor and Hebrew teacher for a group of girls. At our counselors' meetings I said that until now, I had done my best. But now it was my turn to go to Palestine, and to my surprise a solution was found. I joined a group of Hungarian-speaking young people who were about to leave in the framework of Youth Aliya. They were all over eighteen. I took a risk, being two years older, and joined. One of the girls was Tova, with whom I was in contact for many years in Israel until her sudden death, and Adom, a red-headed boy, her boyfriend who went to Kibbutz Negba straight from the boat and joined the fighting in the War of Independence. He was only there for a day or two, when he ran to bring ammunition to a post, and on the way was hit and killed. Adom did not have the opportunity to get to know the country of his dreams.

I waited for our journey to continue. One day we mounted a well-covered truck; the French knew of our coming but asked us to act secretly. We traveled for many hours, leaving Germany in a cold, snowy winter and at night we arrived exhausted and I fell asleep immediately. The following day I woke up to warm spring sunbeams and the sound of birds chirping. I was on the French Riviera. I was truly happy, as if I was already inhaling the air of Palestine. We lived in an isolated house surrounded by a vineyard and an orchard teeming with fruit. We unpacked our shorts and followed the voices we heard speaking in Hebrew. Young people like us were training in marksmanship among the trees, using a wooden flask as their target. An energetic young man with frizzy hair was the counselor. He was the first *sabra* I had ever met. We joined their training in preparation for our expected clash with the British, as we were preparing for illegal immigration to Palestine. One evening we stood on parade, in a three-sided square, in the rain. We were told how to maintain secrecy. We were finally on the move to Palestine. I stood next to my group, holding a Hebrew book that was always with me. That moment and everything that followed moved me so much that I can barely recall that time. A few years later, Yona, a member of my kibbutz, reminded me how she did not associate me with the Hungarian-speaking girls, since I was holding the Hebrew book. We waited for nightfall, walked along a steep slope, each one following in the footsteps of the one before him, down a narrow path, and reached the beach at a secret meeting place near La Suete in the south. A small old boat was waiting for us, bought by the Haganah from Norwegian fishermen. They had refurbished the vessel, fitted it with three-tiered bunks, and packed us in like sardines. The boat that usually served several dozen fishermen was crowded with eight hundred illegal immigrants. We set sail. The smell from the first moment was terrible. From the top tier, to the middle, and down to the bottom, everyone began to vomit. The smell was nauseating. When we entered the straits our boat rocked like a leaf. Everyone was seasick.

I never vomited as a child, not even when I was sick. The lack of air was appalling and we felt we couldn't breathe. I went out on deck and stood near the bow, enveloped in the dark. I heard the waves break and sighed in relief. I didn't feel how the night had passed, I watched the dawn of the second day, and slowly it became light. Next to me I saw one of the Haganah men leaning on the rail. Only later I found out who he was since all of them were traveling under assumed names. He lowered a bucket into the sea and pulled it up with a rope. The water was salty, but with the help of a special soap he gave me that neutralized the salt, I could wash myself, brush my hair, and I felt much better. I became friendly with two *yekke* [German Jewish] families who escaped to England during the war, and who had also reached our ship. Until this day they are members of Kibbutz Ha'maapil, where my sister Chaya lives. When we met them for the first time they told me how they envied me walking around on deck, fresh and clean, while they were lying prostrate, unable to move, a result of their seasickness. Our tiny boat rocked against the waves, even the small ones. At night a British plane flew above, hunting for illegal immigrant ships. After their night patrol, the boys repainted the ship, but in vain—the British recognized us. On the morning of the tenth day of our voyage our boat neared the shore. I saw Mount Carmel. I looked at the mountain, the sun shining on a golden dome, and tears of happiness filled my eyes. Everyone who could, stood up and passionately sang "Hatikvah."

Like the jaws of pincers, two British Tiger-class vessels closed in on us and the battle, for which we had prepared when we were on the French Riviera, began. We threw everything we could lay hands on at the British soldiers—bottles and tin cans. We even managed to hit some of them, but then their rage increased and they directed tear gas at us, and while we were rubbing our burning eyes they flooded us with cold water from huge hoses.

CHAPTER ELEVEN

Cyprus

The battle ended with a few lightly wounded on both sides, but one of our boys was killed. He had no family or friends on the boat and we immediately renamed our vessel "The Unknown Illegal Immigrant." From the moment we encountered them face-to-face, the English were perfect gentlemen. They were very polite, offering us hot drinks and food, but we refused and stood facing them at attention, displaying our pride and singing our national anthem. They did not give up because they did not want to see us starving ourselves, and one officer pleaded with a woman carrying a nursing baby that she should at least drink something for the baby's sake. We were stubborn, unshakable.

The moment came when we had no choice but to cross to the British vessel, but we went slowly, dragging out the transfer process simply to annoy them. The boys actively opposed by lying on the deck and forcing the soldiers to drag them. I couldn't feel the motion of the big ship, I couldn't hear the sound of the waves as it cut silently through the water, and after a short time it dropped anchor off a deserted shore that had no trees or vegetation or even a harbor. We had reached Cyprus, the island of our internment where thousands of illegal immigrants were already housed in big huts like those used by the British soldiers.

Our ship had carried mainly young people, so on our arrival they opened a new camp and from the first moment we counselors called it "The Youth Village" so that the youngsters would not have to use the word "camp," a word that rekindled memories of the terrible past. Life there was organized and the village was like a small, independent country with its own institutions that dealt with all the immigrants' problems. The political parties elected their representative to the various posts and special attention was paid to the youngsters whose schooling had been interrupted.

I went on with my life in Cyprus. Here, too, we were surrounded by barbed wire fences and this took an emotional toll on me. Although the wire wasn't electrified, there were pillboxes—guard-posts—all around it with armed soldiers in them, British, not German. Life bound by the fence and the constant presence of guards aroused terrible memories, but now at least I could see the light at the end of the tunnel.

There were two camps in Cyprus. One was called the "summer camp," whose living quarters were tents, while in the "winter camp," where I was placed, we lived in huts. A small bridge guarded by an armed soldier joined the two camps. As I spoke Hebrew and English, I was chosen to be the liaison between the two camps and enjoyed free passage over the bridge. The permanent guard got to know me and I would give him a big smile in response to his winks as I crossed happily over. Sometimes, hidden in my thick hair and fastened with a bobby pin, I carried an important letter or some money for the Haganah people in the other camp.

On one occasion, as I walked towards the bridge I saw that our plans had gone awry. The usual guard was not there. My heart raced in fear as I approached the unfamiliar officer and gave him the most alluring smile I could muster, while he, cold and indifferent, didn't move a muscle. He didn't even glance at me but called another soldier and ordered him to take me to the nearby town of Famagusta, to a woman officer's home.

I had "won" a free trip, riding in a comfortable car through the streets of the town. We stopped outside a two-story house and, with my escort behind me, we walked to the door. He knocked, I went in, while he stayed outside. I stood in front of the officer, still panting from the effort of climbing the stairs, and instead of asking me to sit down she ordered me to strip. I took off my clothes and stood there in my bra and panties. "Strip, I said!" I removed my underwear—if she wanted it so much she could see me naked. Although I was embarrassed I stood firm. "Everything, I said! Don't you understand?" she shouted.

I understood, completely. I moved slowly to play for time and think of what I would do when she found what I was carrying. I untied my shoelaces, took off my shoes, and placed them by my toes, facing her. Again she shouted at me: "I said everything and that means your socks too!" I didn't respond. I stood pressing my foot to the floor with all my might. The officer bent down and with a look of disgust on her face removed one sock, shook it, and threw it aside, took off the other one, and shook it until the piece of paper fluttered to the floor. She took it, read it, and called my escort to take me back to the camp.

On the way back I was no longer interested in Famagusta's streets and houses; I was thinking about my failure and the damage I had caused. I felt great relief when I heard from those who had sent me that they had thought of every eventuality, and that the message I had carried was coded and so no damage had been caused.

It was spring. I moved to the summer camp, and there I joined one of the kibbutzim, in the hope that my turn for *aliyah* might arrive sooner. We lived in tents right on the seashore, and during the day we wore the absolute minimum of clothing. We didn't work and most of the day was spent swimming in the sea. I was born in a town divided by a river and we had spent a lot of time swimming in the summer. But the first time I went into the open sea with its distant horizon was a daunting experience. The sky reflected in the waves that sometimes reached a height of several meters. The days were hot and I went into the water with everyone else, shivering in fear at first, buffeted by every wave, until I gradually lost my fear.

Among the illegal immigrants in Cyprus there were some very talented people for whom idleness was an alien concept, and who always found something with which to occupy themselves. One of them, Dutzu, was from a Romanian kibbutz and he had wonderful hands. With only a penknife he carved a chess set with its own box that opened on a small simple hinge, and when the box was turned upside down it became a chessboard. To this day I keep it in a drawer together with some small postcards from Shmuel Katz, one of Israel's leading caricaturists, who today lives and works in Kibbutz Ga'aton. In Cyprus he made us beautifully decorated Rosh Hashanah greeting cards, and he was also a music lover who played the violin.

A British patrol boat stood at anchor a few meters away from where we spent our days in the sea and on the beach. Purely out of boredom, we decided to annoy the guards. Some of us swam towards the boat, dived under it, grabbed the keel, and began to rock it. The frightened guard fired into the air —and possibly did something else, he was so scared— while we swam back the way we had come. One day, word got out of some "visitors" who were due to anchor close to the beach, and who must not be discovered under any circumstances. That night we all went out to collect firewood and lit a huge bonfire on the beach, around which we held a *Kabbalat Shabbat* like the ones we had at school and *Hashomer Hatzair*. We sang and clapped and performed a pantomime. The guards' eyes were riveted on what was going on while the boat bringing members of the Haganah to organize our *aliyah* crept close to the shore. The next day, to divert suspicion we introduced them as a soccer team from the other camp who had come to play a match, and thus they were able to mingle among us.

I had never been interested in soccer, but as a result of enforced idleness we all went to the football pitch for the match between the well-fed British and the immigrants. Not a fair contest by any means. I crossed my fingers for our boys, but when I saw the first one trip and suffer a kick from a British soldier, I left, hurt and angry. The result was, of course, a foregone conclusion.

There were times when I despaired. I could only think of one thing: When would this end and when would I leave "The Gateway to the Homeland," as the Cyprus camps were called. I stood by the notice board on which there was a list of immigrants whose turn for *aliyah* had come. The arrangement was perfectly logical—the passengers on the first ship that had come to the island would be the first to leave for Palestine. I had to find a way of bringing my *aliyah* forward.

I looked at the list and saw that a name had been crossed out. I didn't bother to find out why. I simply wrote my name in its place and then spent two days with a woman who was among those whose turn had come. I wanted to know how she had come to Cyprus and to my good fortune she willingly told me every detail, from the time she had boarded the ship to the present. I listened to her like a diligent student. I also asked her about details she hadn't mentioned but which I felt were of great importance, such as what kind of food she had eaten on board the ship, or how many Haganah people accompanied her group. I memorized all these details and it was a good thing that I did. I knew that everything hinged on passing the test.

Each movement had its own quota of immigrants and each representative zealously guarded his movement's interests and *aliyah*. I went into a big tent where the all the representatives were seated. They asked me questions and I answered them with information I had gleaned from my friend. "Please tell us what the weather was like on the journey." It was all over. I was caught out. I wasn't prepared for this question, but I knew I had no choice and without a moment's hesitation I said, "When we left Germany it was very cold, and then it began to rain or sleet, or hail, maybe snow." I had guessed right and passed the test. I was so happy that I didn't know what to do with myself.

To my great sorrow and even greater disappointment, my joy was short-lived. That evening one of the older counselors came to see me and asked me to give up my place to a woman in the advanced stages of pregnancy who very much wanted to have her baby in Palestine. Could I refuse? This time it was even harder to wait and hope for my turn to come. But it came quicker than expected.

I joined a *Hashomer Hatzair* group who had chosen the name "The First of May," some of whom later reached Kibbutz Yas'ur and others went to Kibbutz Ga'aton. My great day arrived. We boarded a British ship and after a short voyage she docked in Haifa. From the port I had another short journey to Atlit where a big transit camp for new immigrants was situated. Some immigrants had been there for many months because the country was simply not prepared for mass immigration. I was there for only two days, and although life in the transit camp was well organized, I just didn't have the strength to wait any longer. I approached one of the people in charge and told him that I had a brother at Kibbutz Ma'anit who knew I was coming and was expecting me. I was released immediately and was given an orange for the journey. At Atlit we were given an orange a day and this was the first time I had ever seen one. As I knew nothing about oranges I picked the biggest one, but I paid for my enthusiasm with disappointment. I didn't know that a big orange has a very thick peel.

CHAPTER TWELVE

Israel

I traveled by bus from Atlit to Hadera. The road passed close to an Arab village and for the first time I saw village boys throwing rocks at us. At Hadera the bus driver accompanied me to a taxi and "translated" my request to the driver to take me to Kibbutz Ma'anit. The Hebrew I spoke upon my arrival was very different from the Hebrew spoken in Israel.

I got off at the kibbutz entrance, walked for several minutes, and met one of the members to whom I introduced myself as Eliezer's sister. He welcomed me warmly, left his backpack on the road and came over to show me the right direction. I stopped in my tracks. "What's the matter?" he asked.

"You left your backpack on the road, and what if someone steals it?"

This was my first lesson in kibbutz life—there were no thieves nor did the kibbutzniks know the meaning of the word. We approached the dining room. I rubbed my eyes to make sure I wasn't dreaming. Near the dining room there were large sacks of oranges. Some of the oranges had fallen out and were lying on the ground. One of the members walked me to the chicken-house where my sister-in-law Pnina worked. She was killed some thirty years later together with her daughter Ada'leh in an accident on the Wadi Ara road.

Pnina, her thinning hair covered with a kerchief, was overjoyed to see me. After we both calmed down she told me that Eliezer wasn't home and would return only in the evening or late at night, after he finished his work.

I was happy to be with them in their home.

I followed Pnina to the small wooden house in which they lived. She went to great trouble to indulge me and later Eliezer returned home. I was jubilant to finally be with them.

There was a great deal of tension in the Jewish community in Palestine at that time and we didn't know what the future had in store for us. My brother, who had studied medicine in Prague, completed his studies in Beirut with the support of the Palmach. He had a driver and a jeep and went from one village to the next organizing clinics and providing first aid. Tension in the country was growing daily.

After our moving reunion he invited me to join them at the table. I couldn't keep my eyes off the large green egg that he divided in two. He removed a huge pit and with a great deal of flair mashed the green-white contents on a piece of bread. "Take some, Rachel, taste our Garden of Eden fruit, you've never tasted anything like it before." From the first minute the "fruit" aroused my suspicion—what kind of fruit does one spread on bread? When I was a child I would eat watermelon or grapes with bread, but to spoil a good piece of bread with a piece of fruit that is neither sweet nor sour? Years went by before I decided to taste it, and since then avocado has become my favorite delicacy.

Despite hard times in the country in general and in the kibbutz in particular, the kibbutz members embraced me into their family with a warmth that is hard to describe. Despite the hard times in the kibbutz they didn't let me go out to work for the whole first week. They told me that I needed a rest and pampered me with delicacies. One of my brother's neighbors worked at the Galam factory that produced halva. When he heard that I had never eaten it, each kibbutz member brought me a different kind, just to taste. My sister-in-law's kitchen was filled with halva. One day, several members invited me to come and visit the factory. It was nearby so I took a walk over there and saw the large vats in which the halva was boiling and spilling over the sides, flies swarming around it—and from that moment my love affair with halva came to an abrupt end.

The mobilization of kibbutz members by the Haganah and the Palmach reduced the number of available workers. The members of Ma'anit worked hard by day—from dawn until dark—and then guarded the kibbutz through the night. Ma'anit was surrounded by Arab villages. Kibbutz members stood at guard duty in posts that surrounded the kibbutz; a man would stand with his gun—at that time we had few weapons—and next to him a woman, whose job was to run through the trenches (by then the kibbutz had a network of trenches) with messages for the person in charge who would always be in the dining room at the center of the kibbutz.

Before I went to sleep after my first day at the kibbutz my sister-in-law showed me a large gong and stick hanging near their home. She explained to me that in a time of danger someone would bang the gong and that was the alarm. If we heard this sound at night we had to run quickly to the shelter in their son Yair's kindergarten. Without even thinking I told Pnina that I had finished running away. I did not care about the Arabs or their shooting, I would not budge nor would I get out of bed. The next day I was ashamed of myself.

On my first morning in the kibbutz I left the room and saw a group of small children taking a walk with their *metapelet* [care-giver]. I was angry at myself for being so selfish and thinking only about my own needs. I worked in the kitchen and at night went on guard duty. Many of the members asked the work organizer to arrange for them to go on guard duty together with me. Most of them had come from Czechoslovakia or Poland, had lost their families, and wanted to hear from me what had really happened in the Holocaust. I felt the need to unburden myself and spoke freely. While I was on duty one evening I saw silhouettes. I told the guard and when he saw them he raised his gun and sent me off to the dining room to notify the person in charge. I ran through the trenches with all my might. My quick actions saved the Haganah boys who were returning from training, but had forgotten to notify the person in charge—it was a miracle that saved them from tragedy.

I reached Palestine in September 1947, and was catapulted straight into the War of Independence. One morning, while my brother was in the communal shower and I was on the other side in the women's shower, we suddenly heard firing from the direction of the nearby Arab village. My brother told me to drop everything, go out through the window, and run quickly to the trenches since bullets had hit the shower door.

My brother knew of my love for Palestine and invited me to join him on his journeys through the country. I went with him and was amazed at how well he knew every inch, from his early Palmach days when they would walk the length and breadth of the country. He pointed out every Jewish settlement that we passed by name, and every adjacent Arab village. I listened but didn't remember a thing. I was extremely tense, seeing only my brother's hands quickly hiding his gun when we approached the British policemen, and quickly taking it out when we neared an Arab village.

Tension rose. Children and mothers were evacuated to Pardess Hanna and those who remained were under the command of the security officer.

The kibbutz was networked with communication trenches, but they were only deep enough to cover us to the shoulders, and we would bend over when we walked in them.

During the day I worked in the kitchen but by that time we weren't doing any cooking. Some of the women would make sandwiches for the soldiers and our members at the guard posts. Once, while preparing these sandwiches, the dining room took a direct hit from a shell that exploded against one of its walls, leaving a huge hole. We weren't hurt because we were on the other side. We hurried to the trenches and at precisely that moment the next shell whizzed over our heads and landed right near me. It crashed against the rock on the side of the trenches but no one was hurt. My face and hair were completely covered in yellow gunpowder.

When I came to Ma'anit I knew it was only a way station from which I would look for my own kibbutz, one that would suit my aspirations, a kibbutz "from scratch," that I could build with my own two hands.

I left Ma'anit but for many years continued to maintain contact with my first home in Israel. Until this day I have a soft spot for Ma'anit and fondly remember their warm welcome despite the hard times. When I went to Givat Haviva to participate in one of the courses held there, I would skip one of the discussions or lectures and visit my friends in Ma'anit who had supported me when I was a newcomer.

I left Ma'anit encouraged and energetic, hoping to realize my dream. I looked for a kibbutz whose members were about my age. I visited Ha'ogen, which seemed very suitable but what convinced me to leave was the Hungarian language that could be heard all over. I said thank you and goodbye. I came to Israel to speak Hebrew.

I heard that there was a group in Hadera waiting to found a new kibbutz. Their temporary name was "Kibbutz Eretz Yisraeli D." Among its members were Yona and Meir Blustein, of blessed memory, with whom I had been in Cyprus where we met at counselors' meetings. I came to Palestine together with them on the same illegal immigrant ship. Yona invited me to come to their kibbutz for a trial period.

A year after I arrived in Israel I reached Kibbutz Yakum. Here is where I met the love of my life, my dear husband Ze'ev, my partner in life for better or for worse, and here is where we built our home and raised our family.

We lived like most of the people in the kibbutz and outside it, with the ups and downs that life dictates. We are appreciative of each day we have together.

When I talk, write, or think about Kibbutz Yakum I have to mention Hannah, blessed be her memory, and Fiska—Shmuel Firstenberg. When I arrived at the kibbutz, Fiska was the kibbutz secretary and head of the building branch. They received me in their small house, in a building that we used to call a *betonada*. They had an infant girl named Ruthie who is now a grandmother. I felt like an older daughter to them. Only those who have lived without a family for years can appreciate what that means.

We have suffered great pain for many years. Only the fact that Ze'ev and I are together and have one another, has given us the strength to continue. Our only son Danny was killed in the Yom Kippur War when he was only twenty-four. We were stunned at his early death, and didn't know how to muster the strength to carry on. Our two daughters and granddaughter Tal, who lost her father when she was only eleven months old, were our reason for continuing. But how?

Our granddaughter Tal lived with her mother Ofra our daughter-in-law, in Beersheba, far away from us. Once a month we took a driver from the kibbutz and visited them. When we returned from our visit we would impatiently await the next one. I used to write stories in rhyme and send them to Ofra to read to Tal, and when Tal grew older and learned to read I wrote her letters. I wrote these letters with tears in my eyes, most of them I kept and still have today.

On our return from one of our visits I took out a notebook. I wrote three lines on the opening page:

"For Tal
When she grows up
And asks about her father."

I wrote about the father whom she never knew. Ze'ev and I knew that, during their short-lived marriage, Danny had not told Ofra about his childhood. I wrote about Danny when he was little and very mischievous, of his love of animals, how he once found an injured jay, took care of it until it got better, and then freed it. I told her also about what a good brother Danny was to his two younger sisters. I showed the notebook to my daughters and they both added memories of their own. I decided that when Tal was eighteen we would show her the notebook. We celebrated her birthday in Beersheba and presented it to her. She wanted to read it and I left it with her. That is all she has of her father Danny. That book was the beginning of my writing.

One month before Tal's first birthday, during the Yom Kippur War, our Danny fell. He was an officer and rushed to save his soldiers, many of whom were wounded by a shell that hit a nearby armored personnel carrier loaded with ammunition. While helping others and evacuating the wounded, Danny was killed. He was awarded a citation that was given to his wife and daughter.

Danny loved people and nature. He was extremely attached to the kibbutz, loved by the children, and at times worked as a *metapel* in the kindergarten when there were no women to do the job. In our family Danny was our beloved only son. When our daughter Idit was a young girl, she would share with Danny the feelings she couldn't share with us. For little Carmit, Danny was a god.

Once when Danny was on a sapper's course in the army, he gathered cyclamen bulbs after an explosion in a training area. He brought them home and planted them near his home in the kibbutz. After his death we took some of the bulbs and planted them near our house, in Ze'ev's sculpture garden, and every winter Danny's cyclamen blooms.

As I grow older, memories of my parents' home have stimulated my writing. When I reached a difficult chapter in my life and felt I could not write anymore, I would write an innocent love story, in order to relax. When I had completed seventeen short stories, they were published by the Yaron Golan Publishing Company, entitled *Therese*. Most of the stories in the book deal with different aspects of love. Two stories are personal, one about my brother Shlomo who disappeared; in the other, "The First Radio in the Kibbutz," I wrote about my life here at home.

This, my fourth book, is the story of my life, entitled "Earrings in the Cellar" to commemorate one of my last moments at home with my mother.

Danny and Edit playing Chess, 1959

My family, 1968

Danny and his two sisters Edit and Carmit, 1972   *Danny in the army, 1969*

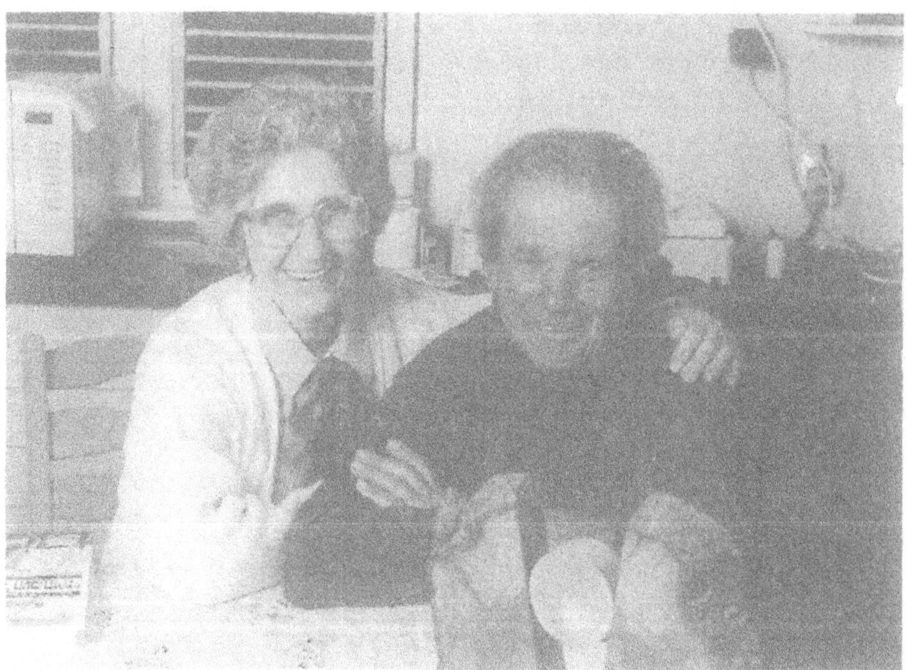

Zeev and me today